THE
FIRST-YEAR
PRINCIPAL

Peter A. Hall

ScarecrowEducation
Lanham, Maryland • Toronto • Oxford
2004

A Scarecrow Education Book

Published in the United States of America
by Scarecrow Press, Inc.
An imprint of The Rowman & Littlefield Publishing Group, Inc.
4501 Forbes Boulevard, Suite 200, Lanham, Maryland 20706
www.scarecrowpress.com

PO Box 317
Oxford
OX2 9RU, UK

British Library Cataloguing in Publication Information Available

Library of Congress Cataloging-in-Publication Data
Hall, Peter, 1971–
  The first-year principal / Peter Hall.
      p. cm.
  Includes bibliographical references.
  ISBN 1-57886-108-X (pbk. : alk. paper)
  1. First year school principals—United States. 2. School management
and organization—United States. I. Title.
LB2831.93 .H35 2004
371.2'012—dc22   2003023613

∞™ The paper used in this publication meets the minimum requirements of
American National Standard for Information Sciences—Permanence of Paper
for Printed Library Materials, ANSI/NISO Z39.48-1992.
Manufactured in the United States of America.

CONTENTS

APPENDIXES: FORMS TO HELP THE FIRST-YEAR PRINCIPAL

INTRODUCTION

The quality of a person's life is in direct proportion to their commitment to excellence, regardless of their chosen field of endeavor.

—Vince Lombardi, Hall of Fame football coach

Welcome, folks. The following text is a compilation of information, advice, strategies, and anecdotes regarding my first year as a principal. Quite simply, the principal is the most influential person in education today.

My intended audience is varied yet distinct. I have written this book for those of you who are currently first-year principals looking for a kindred spirit with whom to commiserate; those of you who are seeking gainful employment as a first-time principal, whether you are a vice principal, dean, preservice administrator, department head, or teacher; those of you who are students in graduate-level school administration programs; and those of you who are simply curious as to why principals rank a close second to American presidents in growing gray hair.

Now, I feel it apropos to offer a disclaimer right from the onset: I am writing this as a first-year principal myself. I do not have the luxury of several years' experience to reflect and apply the wisdom that comes with it. I am not looking back on my first year from the eve of retirement; I am not tainted by melancholy, nor do I sneer with cynicism. I may portray a brash naïveté, which may even border on idealistic idiocy. Some things I clearly do not know, as I have yet to experience everything. I simply have what you will read in the pages that follow: tales from the trenches, my ideas, and my approaches. Some have worked; some have failed. I hope that you read my impressions and share in my passion. I will suggest and share, with neither secrets nor a hidden agenda.

What I have included may shock you, or it may bore you. The stories may sound familiar, or they may seem better suited for left field. These are the true stories of my first year as a principal, and I have included my honest assessments, revelations, and insights. My hope is that each of you will find bits and pieces meaningful; those tidbits, suggestions, attitudes, or criticisms may be of help to you as you seek to understand the position of principal.

You may notice that this text is not suited for a scholarly journal. I've written for those, too, but the material isn't nearly as enjoyable. Plus, principals, by nature of their position and personality, read scholarly journals, reports, data analyses, professional texts, and other works laden with technojargon so often that the *Wall Street Journal* seems like a cranial respite. This handbook, rather, is intended to be light reading, though it carries some heavy statements. It is not, mind you, meant to be a comprehensive guide to the principalship. It is designed to supplement any university coursework or preservice internship, for I can tell you with certainty that no three-credit course or sixty-hour drive-by will explain to you exactly what the job entails. So consider this: Whether you read this for personal benefit, for entertainment, or to gather information, my goal is to provide a little something to fit that need.

I have written this book with short chapters and lots of suggestions and stories, in an informal and (I hope) entertaining style that will not interfere with the message. I would appreciate your feedback, too, so feel free to e-mail me at phall@washoe.k12.nv.us, with your constructive criticism, questions, comments, or concerns.

Now go get 'em!

P.S. I wish I had a book like this eleven months ago . . .

THE JOB

It's a great life . . . if you don't weaken.

—Frank Garrity, lifelong school administrator and personal friend

First off, let me explain a bit about why I decided to become a school principal. I have had a variety of positions within the educational community, including recreation leader, substitute teacher, classroom teacher at several grade levels, math and science facilitator, and dean of students. I chose education in the first place to have a positive impact on young people, to help guide young minds, to straighten the errant. Within my positions, my effect on children and their futures has been great. In each class I taught, there was a student or two who really needed something that I could provide—a role model, an inspiration, a motivation, a person who would listen—and at the end of the school year there was usually some tangible evidence that my impact was beneficial. I entered the administrative realm to expand the scope of my influence.

As the principal, you have access to information about every child. Teachers, parents, community members, siblings, and other school personnel come to the principal with concerns, questions, and suggestions for individual children all the time. You, as principal, have the power and the moral obligation to do right by those children. You will know which child is needy for attention, which one needs a pat on the back, which one needs a shoulder to lean on, which one needs a kick in the rear, which one needs you to phone the parents, which one needs a smile or a high five . . . and you can provide them with all of that.

One of the principal's main objectives is to meet the highly complicated needs of diverse children with a variety of life experiences and situations. For the most part, this is a simple process filled with simple acts. It takes some time and some energy; it takes a firm belief that all children are good from the roots up; and it takes a sense of true dedication. As a teacher, I was able to reach two or three children per year, with intense, meaningful impact; as a principal, I have made that number grow into the dozens. And who knows how many of these children will feel the lasting effects of their interactions with Principal Hall when they are teenagers, young adults, and even older adults?

The school principal is quite simply the most influential person in education today. The principal is more than simply the educational leader; the principal plays many roles in a school. As an example, I have borrowed from Deal and Peterson's *Shaping School Culture* (1990). The principal plays eight symbolic leadership roles:

1. *Historian:* probes into the past; discovers challenges, triumphs, and attempted change
2. *Anthropological sleuth:* researches and examines the school culture directly
3. *Visionary:* addresses and refines the school's mission and purpose
4. *Symbol:* defines the style and demeanor of the school
5. *Potter:* shapes the elements of the school culture with an idea of the vision in mind—that is, the "pot"
6. *Poet:* uses words and images to evoke powerful emotional sentiments about the school
7. *Actor:* applies social dramas to reinforce cultural ties within the school community
8. *Healer:* helps in the change process by participating in ceremonies and commemorative events

As you can tell, there is more to this job than having your own parking spot. Each of you reading this has individual dreams, personal goals, and unique talents that you bring to the table. You have your own motivations, your own desires, and your own reasons for what you do. Your job is to determine how your individuality fits into the educational schema. To best accomplish this end, capitalize on your areas of expertise and work on your weaknesses until they, too, become your strengths.

When Michael Jordan first came to the NBA, the knock on his game was that he was weak on defense and that his jump shot was suspect. Mr. Jordan dedicated himself to the betterment of those two aspects, and the results are stunning: not only did his jump shot become one of the most deadly basketball weapons of all time—as he racked up five NBA MVP awards—but he was named to the NBA's All-Defensive First Team a record nine times. He turned his weaknesses into strengths.

More than anything else, being a principal allows you the unparalleled opportunity to make a difference. Whether that difference effects one child or twenty, you know that your life has just exponentially grown in value. That is the reward. Though money, popularity, and power are the rewards generally associated with a principalship, the benefits of this position are truly intrinsic. When you go home at night (sometimes really late at night) and you know that you did your darnedest to improve the lives of children—through education, socialization, motivation, interaction, support, direction, and discipline—that warmth you feel in your heart transcends the perceived glory and tangible paychecks. This is a noble course you travel.

The quote at the beginning of this chapter is a regular saying of my personal friend and administrative mentor Frank Garrity. The comment was usually preceded by a tirade of profanity-laced expletives said between clenched teeth after a particularly difficult parent left his office; after discussing the inappropriate behavior of a staff member; after revealing frustrations with an incorrigible student; after lamenting the incomprehensible action or inaction of the district office; or after displaying the exhaustion resulting from acting in the position itself. The quote was always followed by a smile. Mr. Garrity, a man of stout integrity, knew how to balance the temporary disturbances with the long-term vision. Rarely did he stew over any particular incident; he knew the job was much larger than any single act.

I have a motto: "Always strive to be a better you." Allow me to explain: "Always strive to be a better you" is a philosophical way to approach every aspect of your life. Based on the teachings of the ancient Greek paideia principle, the goal in life is the attainment of one's ultimate potential, across all fronts. Now, the nebulous idea of one's ultimate potential actually expands the closer you get to it. Therefore, one can never actually reach one's true potential, in any aspect of life. A lesser mind might consider this a fruitless chase of the unattainable; the paideia principle, however, stresses that this pursuit is the motivating force. The end result is that one is always progressing, striving, to be better.

Whether this means being a better father, sister, spouse, or soccer coach; having more patience; cooking with more zest; driving with more caution; listening more intently; teaching with precision; getting along with a distasteful colleague; walking your dog faithfully; or whatever you wish to improve, you're constantly working to better yourself. I have adopted this philosophy into most aspects of my life (I still find myself quite intolerant of Yankees fans that remind me that the Red Sox have not won the World Series since 1918, but I'm working on it—okay, maybe I'm not working on that one yet), and I find it professionally invigorating on a daily basis. You will read a bit more about this later, but I feel this way: no matter how well or poorly things are going, they can always get better. Focus, dedicate, and work for betterment.

POINTS TO PONDER

- More than anything else, do right by your students. You have the power to make or break hundreds of children's lives; use it with a positive slant.
- The job of principal is a multifaceted, complicated position. Define your roles as historian, anthropological sleuth, visionary, symbol, potter, poet, actor, and healer (see appendix A for a handy monthly checklist to keep you on track).
- Determine which of those roles or particular skills are your weaknesses. List them. Develop those aspects into strengths.
- Always strive to be a better you. Consider this statement: If this has meaning for you, embrace the concept.

2

ACQUIRING THE JOB

Unless commitment is made, there are only promises and hopes . . .
but no plans.

—Peter Drucker, Austrian author and educator

So you want to be a principal, eh? What have you done to make this a possibility? What are you prepared to do? What can you expect as you submit the paperwork and participate in the screening-and-interview process? What is the course of events that you must travel? These are the questions that are likely rattling around your head as the prospect of becoming a principal draws near and becomes a potential reality. This chapter is designed to prepare you for the onslaught that forms a fairly typical principal-selection process. My experience, naturally, is district specific, but I have tried to siphon out the main aspects of the process, which should end up looking relatively similar across school districts.

First, this process does not begin with a résumé and written application, you know. It begins long before that, back when you first felt that inkling to be a school administrator, when the thought of thirteen-hour days with no lunch first sounded appealing to you for some reason. Yes, your early written evaluations will come into play, but more important than those are the people with whom you have worked, the contacts you have made, the folks from whom you have earned support and respect. The people who end up in your corner are a strong factor in the equation you provide. This is not to say that you have to schmooze and get in with the "in" crowd, but there is a value to establishing and maintaining strong professional relationships with credible professionals within the district. People talk, plain and simple. If you are the type of person that other folks talk about with respect and admiration, this can add wind to your sails.

So how do you recruit and retain the essential people in your corner? I believe this is accomplished through the persistent work in three areas:

Do your job right. Focus on what is in the best interest of the children under your care and your current school organization as a whole. Align your work practice and your decision making with the established school goals. Perfect your craft. At a time when I was dean of students at a neighboring elementary school, a district-level administrator gave me this advice about the prospects of becoming a principal: "No matter what your goals are for the future, stay in the moment. Your job right now is to be the best dean you can possibly be. Despite what your future ambitions may tell you, there is no reason to focus on anything but excelling in your current position." From that point forth, I strove to set a new standard for deans, to boldly go where no dean had gone before—and, true to form, my name became associated with positive results.

Involve yourself in projects beyond your current position. The first area tells you to be the best at what you do, but the second area tells you to do more. What's the deal there? The two can coexist. Being an excellent dean, department head, or classroom teacher does not necessarily eliminate you from participating in district activities, committees, panels, focus groups, or other projects. If you start shirking your job responsibilities to commit to these projects, however, the value of the perceived benefits will erode rather quickly. Nobody wants to hire an individual who is just going to use the new position as a stepping stone. But they will hire an individual who is willing to contribute more, to participate on a grander scale, and to dedicate time and energy to a worthy cause. So seek out opportunities: participate in a wellness survey, request to be a site trainer for the adoption of a new science text, volunteer to score the state-mandated writing exams, offer to speak at a Lions' Club meeting, conduct an action research project in mathematics and share the results at a district-level math facilitators' meeting, or write a grant for a new barcoding system in your school library. Step out of your comfort zone a little bit; trust me, that's good training in and of itself. Plus, it will look good on your résumé, and you'll meet key people along the way.

Be respectful to everyone you meet. When you meet those key people, be respectful at all times. You never know which of these folks will be sitting on the paper-screening committee for the administrative applications. And, believe me, no matter how objective we like to believe these committees are, human element always comes into play. I'm not advocating that you become Joe or JoAnn Brownnoser and go around smooching rump at the district administrator luncheons, and I'm not suggesting that you abandon your moral integrity when you sit and talk with the folks who would rather talk golf than talk kids. All I am recommending is that you be polite, respectful, and considerate of the people with whom you interact. Don't go out of your way to get noticed in a crowd, and don't nod too much and become a yes-man or a yes-woman; listen a lot and speak respectfully. In general, when you offer respect, it will be returned to you.

When you finally stop by the HR department to pick up the administrative application packet (and do go pick it up, it's three-and-a-quarter-minutes of valuable face time!), its weight will seem immediately daunting. Never mind, get to it. Take your time with this set of forms, for they are the keys to the gate surrounding Principal City. Most districts have established a scoring system for the paper-screening process. Points are awarded to applicants for administrative experience, internships, years of teaching experience, variety of positions held (i.e., different grades taught), degrees held, letters of recommendation (and from whom), and activities in which the applicant has participated (see the previous section).

The application should be thorough but not overwhelming, professional looking but not sterile, precise but not hermetic. If you really want the job, type the damn thing. Most hand-written application packets are rejected nowadays anyway, despite your experience and skills. There will most likely be an essay portion, in which you get to describe your goals and explain why you would like to be an administrator. Be specific and candid, but be careful to not let the delivery interfere with the message—I suggest having a colleague or two examine your entire packet prior to submission, just to be sure you are leaving the right impression. Then turn it in personally (again, about six minutes of face time; ask about the timeline and inquire whether all your confidential reference forms have been returned). Now go home and resume your regular schedule, planting daisies and polishing your kitchen utensils. It's out of your hands now; you'll just have to wait.

Wait indeed . . . to be called for an interview! Administrative interviews rarely occur before positions become vacant; so when you do get that call, you will probably know for which position and school. In any event, though you're trembling with anticipation and shock at receiving that call, ask the caller which open position you are in the running for. Write this information down, along with the date and time of the interview itself. Nothing turns off an interview committee more than a no-show, a late arrival, or a candidate who is introduced as follows: "This next lady is the one that had to call back to find out when her interview was. Hello, have you heard of a Palm Pilot? Yeah, she's real leadership material. Hand me that Gameboy, then call her in."

In between the call and the interview, do some research on the open positions. If you can, visit the schools in question. You most likely will not be able to do this during work hours (because you're busy being the best at your current position), but do stop by in the afternoon, weekend, or in the middle of the night with a dark sweatsuit and a flashlight. Get a feel for the building, the grounds, the neighborhood, the clientele. Then head to the Internet to read each school's accountability report. Find out its strengths and weaknesses; know the mascot and the school colors. Determine patterns in test scores and demographic trends. Phone the folks at the district office; call the current administrator or school secretary; dig around a bit. Any information you can acquire will help your cause immensely. Don't eliminate yourself because of ignorance.

When you attend any interview, you must follow a couple of universal rules. First, dress professionally and appropriately, according to the job in question. You're not going to a wedding, so, ladies, forget the hats. And unless you're a gypsy interviewing for head spell caster, lay off the dangling accessories. Gentlemen, leave the cologne in the cabinet. I know your wives tell you it's sexy and powerful, but you're not going to an audition for The Bachelor; *you're going to a job interview. Brush your teeth. Keep your back straight, sit up, maintain eye contact, smile. Don't say "um," and don't imagine all the folks in the room naked. Imagine yourself as a principal and be confident. You got invited to the interview because you deserve to be there . . . right?*

The first interview will most likely include a large committee of district-level folks, representative personnel from each of the open schools, business community people, and, perhaps, current administrators. In my experience, twenty-three people were already seated at a giant meeting table when I walked in the room. As they introduced themselves, my responses were nearly comical: "Hello, welcome, thank you for being here, nice to meet you, hello, how are you, good to see you, thank you, always a pleasure" (ad infinitum). One chairperson will likely ask all the questions, and that individual is usually a district-level administrator. This practice helps keep the interviews uniform and consistent between candidates. Your job, then, is to answer these generic questions with specific evidence to support your responses; furthermore, your job is to direct at least a portion of your energy toward the individuals from the specific school because, durn it, you did the research on those schools and you're not going to waste it. Just be careful talking about at-risk students for school A if school B has the elite, high-socioeconomic population. Keep the mix varied so that no single group starts rolling their eyes—that can be disconcerting.

In a dark back room in the bowels of some district office building somewhere, the collage of people conducting that first round of interviews will meet and discuss your fate. The committee probably conducted four or five interviews per open position, but they did so concurrently, so you're being considered by each school's representative panel. If your name is forwarded to the next round, that means a conversation like this transpired:

District-level administrator: "School M, which of these candidates would you consider to be viable for your site?"

School M spokesperson: "Candidates T, Y, and Z were acceptable."

District-level administrator: "Were there any candidates you would absolutely not accept?"

School M spokesperson: "Candidates R, S, U, W, and X were unacceptable."

District-level administrator: "What about candidate V? You didn't mention that one."

School M spokesperson: "Ah, well, candidate V would be okay."

District-level administrator: "Perfect. May I have my Gameboy back now? You're excused, thank you."

This conversation (or some variation of it) is repeated for each school with an open principalship.

When you get that next phone call inviting you to the second interview, you can rest assured that at least one of the schools did not eliminate you from contention. Schools generally have the veto power, as expressed in the described scenario. Again, if you are feeling brave and can withstand the rubbery knees, ask the caller which schools forwarded your name. That information will help direct your next interview because that interview is with the big guns and you do not want to show up ill prepared.

Most superintendents and school boards will have a question or two unique to their repertoire, something that is meant to catch you off guard to test your on-your-feet mettle. The rest of the interview is designed to get a feel for your leadership qualities, your career ambitions, your interpersonal skills, and your technical expertise. I have compiled a list that may provide you with a starting point for clarifying your thoughts in preparation for the big day. I suggest you go through it carefully and make notes regarding your points of view, experience, ideas, and philosophy. No sense in stammering over a question and acting like it's the first time you've thought of it when you can prepare yourself and deliver a smooth, honest response instead. You'll find the list (with space for your thoughts and responses even—you're welcome) as appendix B.

You will find yourself in a room with members of the local school board or the district superintendent and a small cadre of district officials that form the superintendent's "inner circle," the folks that have earned the supe's trust and decision-making honors. With some good fortune, you will already know one or several of the individuals in the room; that will help. (Did you do work in the second area, involving yourself in projects beyond your current position? If so, you will know someone else in the room.) During this interview, imagine you are a principal. Conduct yourself in that light. Project the image that will make those honchos proud. Can they tell you are principal material? Do the following to convince them that you are principal material indeed.

Speak to the specifics of the schools as you have researched them; be honest in all accounts; be confident in every answer you give; and ask for clarification if a question is confusing. When the interview has concluded, shake each person's hand (no dead fish), maintain eye contact (no winking), thank them for considering you (no blabbering begging), push in your chair (use your hands, not your hips), and exit swiftly (don't trip, don't run, don't skip). Then go back home and fall into your regular routine of rearranging furniture and vacuuming the windowsills. And wait for the call . . .

POINTS TO PONDER

- Put yourself in a realistic position to acquire the job. Recruit people of influence into your corner to support your ambitions. Do this by engaging in three particular areas of emphasis:
  - Do your job right. Be the best at your current position.
  - Involve yourself in extra projects. Volunteer for committees; work on district-level activities; contribute to a worthy cause.
  - Be respectful at all times. Don't burn bridges: you never know which one you'll need to cross some day.
- When you submit your application packet, type it. Be thorough, but succinct, in your responses. Turn in the packet personally, for "face time" in the human resources office; it is time well spent.
- Conduct research on the open positions. Visit the schools with administrator vacancies; log onto their websites; call and talk to people that know about the school and neighborhood. Arm yourself for the interviews. Review the sample interview questions listed in appendix B.
- In the interviews, project confidence. Imagine that you are already a principal and force that image upon your audience. Alleviate any doubt in the interviewers' minds that you would not represent the district well.

3

PREPARE THYSELF

Keep your fears to yourself, but share your courage with others.

—Robert Louis Stevenson

One day you'll wake up with the birds chirping, the sun shining, the flowers blooming, and the coffee percolating, and you'll know it is The Day.

When the district official comes to your school and asks to meet with you, be accommodating. Rejections are generally sent through the mail or conducted on the phone, so a personal visit is a good sign. If you work in a district like mine, you will not be offered the job. You will be designated. I got, "Congratulations, Pete, you're the new principal of Anderson School." Brash as I may be, I replied, "Very well, I accept," although my acceptance was obviously implied in the assignment. Nevertheless, there it is.

There are two natural stages that you will progress through over the following weeks. First, the "Oh, boy!" stage, one characterized by a whirlwind of excitement and energy, smiles, extravagant dinners that you won't be able to pay off for a few months, and a noticeable swagger. Second, you'll hit the "Oh, shit!" stage, one characterized by a glazed look, wobbly legs, and the gaping mouth that rides shotgun with the knowledge that you, novice, are now expected to be the expert on thousands of the best educational practices for some five hundred students, while leading a staff of around fifty . . . and keeping your office looking neat for when your spouse stops by.

Depending on when you got your assignment, you may have some time before the current school year ends—and you certainly have time before your new school year starts—to perform a few preparatory steps. Let's consider these one at a time:

1. Get the building affairs in order. Face it, you are the principal at school X because one of a series of possible scenarios is playing out: the previous principal is moving, transferring, retiring, getting fired, being hospitalized, seeking an easier job as the head of a major corporation, or beaming to Vulcan . . . in one way or another, that principal is leaving! Once the deal is made, you need to ask yourself, How much time and energy is the exiting principal going to spend on the "old job," especially since a "new boss" is entering the picture? (That's a rhetorical question; you don't have to answer it.) You are not the principal that starts next year; you're the principal that starts today! All decisions made with future bearings should belong to you; all planning should include you; and although you need not be present for the day-to-day operation of the building until the conclusion of the current school year, you need to be kept in the loop. How do you stay in the loop? Follow the following steps.

2. Get a feel for the place. Spend some time observing the students, classes, staff, and families; make note of the building routines and schedules; and focus on the climate of the school. In short, get to know the gig. You already did some paper and Internet research during the interview process, so you have a database started; add to it. Review test scores; poke through random student folders; check out the local assessments used for reporting student progress. Then walk through the classrooms—you will already have been introduced to the teaching staff, so you might as well take a minute or two in each classroom to introduce yourself to the students as well. Take a good look around. Walk the grounds during recess, taking note of what the students are engaged with, the quality and quantity of adult supervision, the resources, and the atmosphere. Do the same in the lunchroom. Stop by before and after school to meet some parents and watch the flow of traffic—by foot, bus, skateboard, car, and otherwise. Know what it is that you're going to be dealing with over the next several years.

3. Establish yourself as the authority figure. Let's get one thing clear right away: you are no one's friend; you're the boss. That is not to say you cannot be friendly, but be wary of those individuals that try to reel you in right away. Initially, make no commitments to anything but excellence, a focus on student achievement, and continuous improvement. Anything less vague will bite you in the rear. Practice saying "We'll see," "It depends," "I'll decide that later," and "That's a good question." That's how you should answer every teacher's question, every parent's request, and every student's plea.

Measure your comments, and trust no one—get to know the players before selecting those for your "inner circle." And when you create that inner circle, make it strong. I would suggest keeping that inner circle tight for a while, including only your dean or vice principal and maybe one trusted, loyal teacher. Run your thoughts, visions, and ideas by them. Ask for input, but make the decisions yourself. As for the other members of your staff, keep them at a healthy, professional distance for a while. Remember, you don't really know everyone's existing reputation, everyone's work habits, whether one complains mercilessly in the staff room and praises effusively in the office, why each is in the profession, what everyone's agenda may be for making a certain request—so be wary.

At the onset of my tenure, I was labeled "unfriendly" (I think it was more in contrast to the exiting principal than anything else), but I was businesslike nevertheless. I was careful not to buddy up to anyone, not to extend favors or offer preferential treatment. They were all equals, and I was the boss. At least until the end of the current school year, I would allow the status quo to continue. But I was setting the stage for my emergence as the principal, the new sheriff in town.

4. Begin to build relationships with your personnel. Now that everyone realizes you're the boss and that you won't topple, you can make some headway with the staff. I suggest you meet with each individual . . . individually. Yes, it takes time, especially if you want to do it right, but you didn't work to get this job so that you could slack off, did you? Make a schedule that includes early-morning, late-afternoon, and even weekend meetings . . . the existing staff will want to get a piece of you one-on-one just as much as you would like to chat with each individual one-on-one. Have the secretary keep the schedule and allow teachers to sign up at their leisure. Then meet with each one. What an opportunity to get to know the players, to get their feel for where the school is headed and what its needs are!

Ask questions about their background, their personal goals, their wishes for the upcoming school year; and don't be afraid to be specific. Ask some tough questions, such as "Why do you think the reading scores for ESL students have actually decreased over the past three years?" or "What do the conversations in the staff room generally sound like?" Ask about schedules, special events, staff meeting protocol, parking privileges—you name it. You won't learn if you don't ask.

I spent literally dozens of hours, but I met with every individual that worked in that school: from the kitchen staff to the clinical aide, from the head custodian to each classroom teacher. I found this to be an excellent time to relay some of my expectations to the personnel. If you have a message to send, do it in this arena so that it's not a big surprise in your startup staff meeting (to be explained in the following).

5. Cultivate your vision for your new school. Be careful here. If you are fortunate, the school will have had an established vision, which you will not want to completely eradicate while implementing your own. After determining the school's established vision and goals, you can begin the progression from the previous vision to the current—that is, yours. Take some time with this. In chapter 5, you'll read more about how to temper your enthusiasm and curb your natural tendency to rip up the floors and change carpeting, but I can tell you this now: it's not terribly important that you begin to share your vision with the staff right away, at least the nitty-gritty nuts-and-bolts parts of it. Change is, by nature, a frightful thing. What is important—vital, essential, critical, necessary, imperative, crucial (read: something you kinda-oughta focus on)—is that you have a clear picture of where your school will be in four years and how you are going to help it get there.

The startup staff meeting is the one that keeps you awake every night for the eleven days prior to it. It's the one that makes you buy extra antacids for the last week. It causes you to forget to feed the pets in the morning; it makes you oblivious to spousal requests to pick up certain groceries on the way home; and it contains some ingredient that teaches you to talk in your sleep.

When preparing for this meeting—which, by the way, is at the end of the summer and is the first get-together for the entire staff—consider a few things. First, your agenda is not the only agenda. It's important, but it's just a portion of the *orden del día*. The teachers will want some social time to renew their friendships, talk about their summers, and whisper comments about the new principal. Set aside the initial forty-five minutes as a nonmandatory breakfast social. For it, go buy fruits, juices, yogurt, bagels, and some donuts (not too many donuts: high-carbohydrate, high-sugar foods won't provide the energy boost needed to survive the startup meeting). Make the table pretty. When those forty-five minutes are up, start the meeting. It's important to let the folks know that 9:15 AM means 9:15 AM, not 9:17 or 9:21. Time is money: once it's spent, it's gone, so spend it wisely.

The written agenda is important. Consult with your inner circle as to the topics you should include. (In appendix G, I've included a sample belief system survey to give to your teachers during the meeting, to help you get a feel for their attitudes.) Try to keep the written parts of the agenda brief so that it doesn't appear overwhelmingly aggressive. If a particular topic does not absolutely have to be discussed on that first day, table it. If you have handouts, either distribute them in collated stacks or provide sorted piles next to the sign-in table at the entryway. What you discuss in that first meeting is as important as how you discuss it (appendix C is a copy of my startup staff meeting agenda). Believe me, and this is not meant to make you more nervous than you will already be, every word you speak, every smile, every grimace, every hesitation, your body language, your hand gestures (careful here!), your confidence, your voice tone, your clothing, hair, nails, setup of the room, everything . . . will be scrutinized. Because you don't want to lose the message in the delivery, I suggest that you approach every aspect of this meeting as businesslike, friendly, and focused. If a staff member goes off on a tangent, don't be afraid to redirect: "I'm sorry, this is not the appropriate forum for your concerns. Hold that thought, it's an important thought, but let's talk about that another time. Now, back to the checkout procedure for PE equipment . . . "

POINTS TO PONDER

- Understand from the get-go that when you are awarded a principalship, you will experience both the "Oh boy!" stage and the "Oh shit!" stage. Awareness of how you feel, and that your feelings are entirely normal, is crucial.

- Assume the roles and duties of the principal as soon as you receive your appointment. Whether the incumbent wants to admit it or not, it's now your school, and you are ultimately responsible for its direction. Follow these steps to prepare yourself:
  - ○ Get the building affairs squared away. Stay in the loop.
  - ○ Get a feel for the place. Start spending as much time as you can in the building. Observe teachers and students; scour test scores; and familiarize yourself with the established culture and routines.
  - ○ Establish yourself as the boss. Remain businesslike, offer no favors, and make no promises. Ask for information and input from the key players, but make all decisions yourself.
  - ○ Build relationships with staff. Meet with each member of your staff individually. Listen to them, share your ideas, and learn their positions.
  - ○ Cultivate the vision. Begin to envision where your school is and where you would like it to be in four years . . . then figure out how to get it there.
- In your startup staff meeting, the written agenda is important. Keep it brief. Your manner, presence, and responses to questions are vital. Maintain a businesslike approach; keep the meeting focused; and, remember, you're in a room full of professionals. See the sample startup meeting agenda in appendix C.

LIGHTNING STRIKES

"Toto, I've a feeling we're not in Kansas anymore."

—Dorothy, in the 1939 movie *The Wizard of Oz*

The principal position is nothing like being a department chair, a dean of students, or even a vice principal. It's a whole new world. I don't mean to slight any university's administration and educational leadership program, any preservice internships, any on-the-job training programs, or any activities that leave a future administrator confident in his or her preparation for the job, but no matter how ready you think you are, you're not. Nothing can prepare you for the tsunami of principalship other than getting into it, bracing yourself, and wearing galoshes. Well, yes, reading this book, of course, will help a lot.

Here's a way to compare whatever you have done before the principalship and what you will do during the principalship itself: Your preparation, internships, coursework, assistant principal position, leadership roles, and intestinal fortitude are the equivalent of Bambi. The principalship is Godzilla. Get the picture?

As principal, you have the ultimate responsibility for everything that occurs, exists, or is even considered within, around, or nearby your school facility. The buck stops here, whether you want it to or not.

Whereas a dean of students, a department head, or a committee chair has all the perceived authority that accompanies the position or job title, the definitive accountability for any decision made by the people in those positions rests back in the principal's office. The vice principal can tell a group of teachers that their request is granted for such-and-such, and those teachers can forward the good news to their students; but when the funding doesn't pan out and when the parents start barking, who do you think is going to take the heat?

To take a business perspective on the principalship, one might refer to the job as a combination position of chief executive officer and chief financial officer (CEO–CFO). The principal runs the show (the school-wide educational plan), hires and supervises the personnel (the staff), monitors the factory (the instructional practices), inspects the facility (the school building), accounts to the customers (the students and parents), reports to the parent organization (the school district office), maintains future considerations (the vision), operates the finances (the funding sources, including fund-raisers), and takes on each of the eight roles listed in chapter 1. This is no small undertaking. For me, when I was assigned this gig as principal, I suddenly inherited the full command of five hundred students and fifty staff members, squeezed into a thirty-two-thousand-square-foot facility, with over a quarter of a million dollars in funding to run a comprehensive elementary education plant.

Whether you are a dean of students, a classroom teacher, or a vice principal, you always have aspects of the school operation that you do not need to know. You don't need to know the intimate details of the boiler room, and you don't need to know who handles the roofing contract; you don't need to know which teacher received unsatisfactory marks on her last evaluation, and you don't need to know which teachers attended the literacy training sessions and which still need to make up those hours; you don't need to know how much money is left in the account that pays for substitute teachers, and you don't need to know the deadlines for submitting budget adjustment requests. There is a lighthearted freedom that people in those positions have yet to realize they possess. They can take for granted that if they need to find out that information, they can ask the principal, who darn well better know.

Quite simply, the principal must know everything about everything in the school. Now, you will probably hear from university professors, colleagues, and maybe even principals a statement that sounds like this: "It's okay to say 'I don't know.' That allows your staff to understand that you are just a person, constantly learning and growing, and you have to find out the answer." Ha! It's okay if you don't mind losing a bit of credibility, but what message is the principal really sending if, for example, the principal is sitting in a conversation with several primary-grade teachers talking about emergent literacy, and the principal cannot answer a question regarding phonemic awareness ("Um, gee, well, let me look that up and get back to you"); or, say the principal is approached by a teacher who asks about the district policy on students' carrying electronic equipment to school, and the principal ponders aloud, "It seems like that would be okay, but I guess I could see a problem there, I don't know what the district says, let me check." How much faith will the staff and students have in that leader in the case of a true emergency, in which absolute knowledge is essential to their very survival?

Okay, so that may be a bit extreme, but when it comes to the facts, rules, regulations, and professional knowledge that a principal should have, here is my advice: Know them! If you don't know the policies and procedures, if you lack the foundations of knowledge for the grade levels you now hold charge, or if you are not familiar with the rules of the educational road, take the time to learn them. There is no substitute for not only being the authority figure because of the job title but also being the authority because of your personal knowledge and expertise.

However, in your first year as principal, you will be faced with what feels like a million decision-making opportunities—and not all of them are fact based. The sheer volume of things that cross your path is truly awesome, in the classical sense of the word. Imagine the following (in what seems like one continual voice throughout your day):

"Our clerk doesn't have access to an online computer. Can we get a new bulletin-board in room 12? The clinical aide is trying to nurse several week-old kittens to health after a coyote killed their mother. The special education class needs a new aide, since the last one moved to Scotland. The custodian's pager isn't working, how about getting two-way radios? We've changed the computer lab schedule, does that affect the duty schedule? Should the teachers lock their outside doors during lunch, or can the students duck in to pick up playground equipment for recess? If not, how are the primary students going to carry a ball through the lunch line without spilling their peaches and taco? The air conditioner in the portable building has a hornet's nest in it, that's why it's ninety-seven degrees in here. You have two students in your office for throwing rocks at the neighbor's dog again. The sink in the staff room is clogged. The third-grade teachers need two additional math texts, and who is responsible for tracking down the students after they move if they took a book with them? We may have a witness for the graffiti incident over the weekend. I think that guy picking up his son has alcohol on his breath. How old is this carpet in the office anyway? What are you going to do, boss? What are you going to do?"

Some of these scenarios do not need to be dealt with immediately, and some of them do not even call directly for the principal's involvement. There may not be a right or wrong answer to these issues or questions, and that makes it okay to not be the expert in these circumstances. Here, it is acceptable to respond with "It depends," "We'll see," or "What do you think we should do?" Your credibility and sense of authority are not quite as at-risk here; but I believe any principal's approach to the mundane, the typical, the novel, and the wild, coupled with an ability to make snap judgments and immediate decisions, is what separates the ordinary from the extraordinary. Frequently what teachers would like from the principal is a decision. Right or wrong, they are looking for confidence and personal authority. And if the decision is aligned with the accepted vision of the school and if it is reasonably considered, your stock will rise.

The situations listed here are quite typical, nothing like the exceptional fires that seem to spontaneously combust—for example, a middle-school student who picks fights with sixth-graders and tells the duty teachers to "f— off"; a social services warning of a sexual predator who was recently released from prison and is allegedly on the prowl to snatch his first-grade ex-step-daughter; a pulled fire alarm right before lunch; a fight that broke out and required your physically restraining the student; the after-school program that starts tomorrow, despite the fact that the personnel office still needs requisitions. Face it: the principalship is a busy job. People hit you up for information, ideas, questions, complaints, offers, venting, bickering, praising—you name it. All day, every day, the regular events transpire. Then the crazy stuff hits and the unforeseen events occur. You didn't get into this line of work for the monotony, did you?

POINTS TO PONDER

- Being an assistant principal versus being a full-fledged principal is like Bambi versus Godzilla. Just know up front that the differences between any position you've ever had and the principalship are vast and extreme.
- The principal has the ultimate responsibility for everything that happens in the school building. You are the CEO and CFO. The buck, every buck, stops with you.
- There is a certain amount of professional knowledge, facts, rules, and regulations that the principal should be an expert on. Learn those, know them, and be the expert.
- Brace yourself for the sheer volume of questions, comments, concerns, items, and requests that cross your path. "Be prepared," as the Boy Scouts say, for even the things you have never even heard of before.
- Think ahead. The principal's approach to the novel, and an ability to make snap decisions, is what separates the ordinary from the extraordinary.

5

JUST BECAUSE YOU'RE NEW

"Before y'all get to beaming me up there's a couple of things I want you to understand. First off, you chose me, so you recognize the skills, and I don't want nobody calling me Son, or Kid, or Sport, or nothing like that, cool?"

—Will Smith, as Agent J, in *Men in Black*

When I was first appointed principal, I began to hear the little jibes, those offhand comments about my age. Sure, I was a thirty-year-old first-year principal, but come on. "Here comes the boy," "junior principal," and "the kid" were some of the several statements meant to prod me, I suppose. But when I heard "Who is this, Alex P. Keaton?" I felt enough was enough (you'll remember that Alex was the character played by Michael J. Fox on the television show *Family Ties* and that he was a boyish, tie-wearing overachiever). At our first whole-group gathering prior to the new school year, I was tempted to play the clip from *Men in Black* in which Will Smith's character let Tommy Lee Jones's character know in no uncertain terms that he had heard enough of the age-specific, demeaning comments (see quote at the beginning). However, since the clip contained one colorful word, I opted against it.

Instead, during my opening address to the staff, I told them this: "I understand that I appear to be a young fellow, and to some of you I may actually be young. I have heard all the comments about my age, and some of them amuse me. But we have work to do, so . . . if any of you have any further comments to make for the good of the group, go ahead and share them now." This was followed with what seemed to be a rather lengthy period of awkward silence and furtive glances about the room as the group tried to discern my intent. I finished with, "In that case, let's consider it past history and proceed with our business." It worked. I haven't heard a "young gun" comment since.

However, as a new principal, regardless of your age, you face obstacles simply as a result of what you are: a new principal. As such, you have never done this work before. You have not been here; you have not conquered this. And every single one of the folks on your staff knows this. This is not necessarily bad; it's just a simple fact. There will be two types of personnel working for you during your first year as boss:

1. Folks who are returning. They worked at that school before you got there, and they will continue to work there after your arrival.

2. Folks who are new. They, like you, are fresh faces in your school building, whether as a transfer, a new hire, or simply a result of pure dumb luck.

The second group, most likely formed of employees that you hired or accepted via transfer, knows nothing other than your leadership in that school. They have not worked in a climate other than the one you have established in that building, so they are less likely to compare your decisions, attitudes, beliefs, and interpersonal demeanor with your predecessor. They know you as boss, and they have no other frame of reference with which to waffle their allegiance and understanding of your position as principal.

That first group, however, is the group with which you will likely encounter the most resistance, so it follows that this is where you should exercise planned precision and liberal caution. These are the people who have worked in your school under alternate leadership, perhaps for a year, perhaps for twenty years. They have seen principals come and go; they have watched and experienced the changes in leadership and the methodical swing of the educational pendulum. This may be a generalization, but they are not impressed. You are one more in a series of temporary leaders, placed in a school that was here before you showed up and will be here after you leave; you are in charge of teachers that were here prior to your placement and will last longer than your tenure. You are temporary; they are permanent.

The first challenge in garnering the support of the more ingrained staff members is to demonstrate respect for your predecessor. Make public note of the good results the staff has achieved; praise the prior principal, and mention how difficult it will be to fill "such big shoes." Thank the staff for welcoming you and for working with you as you continue the journey down a common path forged by strong leadership, by a consistent emphasis on quality, and by the existing staff's thorough work ethic. Assure the staff that you are not there to demolish the structure of the school and that you are not interested in overseeing radical changes immediately.

Not only will the current staffers have a heightened sense of anxiety, which is natural in any organization after a change in leadership, but you must be wary of this at all times. Even with an ineffective principal, most teaching staffs will have settled into some semblance of a comfort zone, one that that walks hand-in-hand with an understanding of that principal's expectations, routines, and expected behaviors. When the principal changes, that comfort zone disappears: the expectations change; the routines are altered; and the expected behaviors are unknown. It takes a while to reestablish those facets of the job, and you cannot accomplish this without a concerted effort to value and notice the previous culture and the inherent changes forthcoming.

During my first whole-group startup staff meeting, I had the teachers "interview" each other and introduce their partners to the group. One teacher, after talking with an established veteran teacher, introduced her as such: "This is Mrs. So-and-so. She has been teaching for fourteen years, and she has already outlasted four principals." After the nervous giggles of the crowd subsided, I felt fifty pairs of eyes on me, awaiting my reaction. I simply smiled and said, "And she has made a point of that." Then, turning to Mrs. So-and-so, I quipped, "Thank you for sticking around." I certainly did not take this personally; it was inevitable. Throughout the course of my first year, however, my support and energy have made an impact. I recently received a note from this teacher, stating "Remember that first day? Well, you are truly the best! Thanks!"

Along those same lines, it is important to temper your enthusiasm and to curb your temptations to leap headlong into the water, damning the sharks, mines, and unseen coral reefs below. In simpler words, start slow. Although you have a million ideas and a limitless well of enthusiasm and though you cannot wait to get into the fray and start leaving your mark on your new school, you must have patience. After establishing yourself as the authority figure and leader (see chapter 3), demonstrating praise and respect for those who came before you, and after validating the professional practices the staff has engaged in over the past few years, go sit down. You don't need to rush toward your vision yet.

It takes a while to establish a shared vision, one that the entire staff embraces as a common goal; and it takes time to refine the vision and lay out the path toward reaching it. Keep in mind, also, that a typical tenure of a building principal is three to five years and that any quality vision for a school is a long-term objective. None of this is done overnight, and not all of it even needs to be addressed in the first six months of a new principal's first year. Take your time, relax, soak it in, get a feel for what's going on, refine the vision in your own mind, then start disseminating the good word. If you will permit me to join two common sayings in an uncommon manner, the following rings true: Patience is golden.

Right off the bat, your experience and qualifications will be in question. This triples in severity if you are, or appear to be, under forty-five years old. You do not have to pass out your résumé and outline your curriculum vitae in your startup meeting to convince your staff that you are deserving of the job title. Obviously, the folks at the district office were convinced, and, for any outright confrontations about your qualifications, all you need reply with is, "I earned this position on my own merits. I appreciate your interest in my background and accomplishments, and I'm sure some day this will be a topic of conversation in which I will participate. However, as for now, we have a job to do, so let's get to it." That might squelch some of the blatant questioning in public, but it certainly will not alter the fact that every decision you make, every comment you utter, every meeting you hold, and every directive you provide will be scrutinized.

If you come to grips with this from the onset, it will not be a terrible surprise when one of your first decisions will be the subject of heated debate and a raving teacher in your office. If you held true to your vision and made the decision based on the best interests of the students, you have little to fear. As long as you can justify your actions beyond any reasonable doubt, you're golden. Furthermore, this mind-set betters your position for being patient and not making earth-shaking decisions early in your tenure.

When the dust clears, you will find yourself in the midst of a whirlwind, but you'll be prepared for it. You will understand the nature of the beast, and you will be spared the exasperating torrent that wreaks havoc on the ill prepared. And as time creeps forward and the school year begins to take shape, you can begin to mold your new school within your vision and isolate areas of immediate concern. This is where you take your second deep breath, find a quiet place on a Saturday afternoon, and prioritize. To keep it simple and within four syllables: Pick your battles.

While in the principal's chair, remember that every decision matters. The decision to even make a decision (or not) is an important decision. My recommendation prior to making any decision is to measure the cost–benefit of each proposed option. Consider all alternatives and reflect on their ramifications. As you are a new principal and as every decision will be scrutinized anyway, it makes sense for you to engage in some thorough consideration before making a final decision. If you equip yourself with this intensive forward-thinking, preemptive mentality, coupled with the complete understanding of how the apples will fall if you shake the tree, then the results will not surprise you. However, when I write, "pick your battles," I'm not simply referring to calculating the cause-and-effect relationships harbored within decisions. This has more to do with determining whether you are willing to expend the time, energy, finances, and human gusto to follow each course you have chosen.

If the copy machine is out of toner, you order more. That is a simple decision. When the issues begin to involve personnel, however, you will need time for reflection and analysis. The placement of the teachers' mailboxes, the direction of the student flow through the lunch line, and the assignment of recess duties are relatively simple subjects, although they include that irascible human element and therefore require a certain degree of investigation. Issues that involve teacher evaluation, legal issues regarding teacher conduct, the reclassification of personnel positions, the organization of the school day, the time and agenda of staff meetings, and staffing allocation issues are topics that deserve the utmost consideration before any type of decision.

Any type of personnel action has associated costs. What costs are you willing to pay to settle the tumult in your professional gut? Some things you know are not working as efficiently as possible, and some people you know are not as effective as they could be . . . but do you want to take them on? It is not an easy task balancing your professional integrity ("Children deserve the very best, and they are not getting it with this person; therefore, I need to make it change") versus the cold-hearted reality of the school setting ("Any whiff of principal-versus-teacher sets off alarms in all corners of a school and extends beyond the walls to the neighborhood, district, teachers' union, and so forth"); nevertheless, it is vital to your success and survival. Pick and choose your battles; engage in combat only for the right reasons (the best interest of the kids); and limit your ensnarlments to what you can realistically handle while still running the rest of the show.

By the way, in response to Will Smith's character's diatribe during the scene from *Men in Black*, Tommy Lee Jones's character replied, "Cool, whatever you say, Slick, but I need to tell you something about all your skills. As of right now, they mean precisely dick," and he proceeded to show young Agent J that he was entering into a world about which he really knew nothing at all.

There's a parallel here that is too powerful to ignore, but I'll let you draw your own conclusions.

POINTS TO PONDER

- You are new at this. Accept that fact, and understand that every new experience entails a steep learning curve, for both the principal and the staff, the latter of whom forms two groups:
  - *New folks:* With these people, your leadership is all they have known at this school, so you have some immediate support. Be careful not to alienate them because they're new; their support is vital.

○ *Returning folks:* With this group, everything you do will be compared against your predecessor. Here is where you want to be cautious and precise, offer support and praise, and garner their support and approval. Utilize their strengths and make a point of them.

- Start slow; don't come in with guns blazing. Nothing strikes more fear in teachers' hearts than a new leader who immediately implements strategies and ideas. Get a feel for the current before trying to swim against it.
- Pick your battles. Not everything has to be perfect right away, so don't try to bull your way to perfection. Measure the cost versus the benefit of each proposed action, and engage in combat for only the right reasons. Only bite off what you can chew.

6

HIRING THE RIGHT FOLKS

Everybody can be great . . . because anybody can serve. You don't have to have a college degree to serve. You don't have to make your subject and verb agree to serve. You only need a heart full of grace. A soul generated by love.

—Dr. Martin Luther King Jr.

Your personnel will make or break you. Good teachers with positive attitudes and an excellent work ethic will likely make you look like an effective leader. Poor teachers sharing negative comments and slouching on the job will likely make you appear weak and ineffective. So which comes first, the effective leader or the effective staff? Luckily, the principal can be the deciding factor either way. This chapter provides some assistance in ways to ensure the hiring of the right people, and the following chapter tackles the challenges of supervision and evaluation so that you can cultivate an effective teaching staff.

Before we jump right into the deep pool of hiring, let's take a second to adjust our goggles and check the water temperature. Any effective administrative program in a credible school of education will teach you that hiring is the fourth step in the process, following recruitment, interviewing, and background checks. The simple, widely accepted approach to those three steps is to casually stroll into the human resources department to peruse applicant files, call several people in for interviews, ask them why they want to work in a school, read their letters of recommendation, and go with the gut to pick the winner.

Ha! Don't ever take it that lightly. Try this six-step approach before hiring anyone:

1. Actively recruit. As soon as you know you have (or are going to have) an opening, go find a cache of highly qualified candidates. Attend job fairs, visit teacher education programs at your local universities, talk to your colleagues and peers, and seek out the all-stars.

2. Scour the applicant files. Don't just look casually or peruse. Scour. Search high and low for the skills and abilities you need for the open position in question. If you're looking for a primary-grade teacher, look for extensive evidence of the applicants' knowledge in teaching beginning reading and cognitive development. Scour.

3. Involve the right people. During the interview process, assemble your interview team with care. Discuss your objectives beforehand with that team. Agree, or at least understand, what skills and traits you demand for the position.

4. Make the interview matter. Select interview questions carefully, and ask them clearly. To get your applicants' best and consistent answers, ask the questions uniformly. (See appendix D for sample interview questions.)

5. Scrutinize the top candidate. Just because an applicant has impeccable paperwork and performs gloriously in an interview (and brings a gift of a rare Jerusalem tulip) doesn't mean that person is necessarily the right person for the job. There is always something you can glean from talking directly with supervisors and coworkers. Do the digging. You may uncover skeletons in the closet, and you may find rose petals framing the image. The hour or two you spend investigating a candidate will be worth your time in the long run.

6. Eliminate vacillation. Before offering the job (assuming you have approval from the human resources department to offer the job), be sure. Know from the cockles of your heart to the tips of your toenails that this person is the right person for the job. If you have any hesitation whatsoever, balk. Wait. Stall. Interview others. Do more digging. Go for a walk, buy a pair of horn-rimmed glasses, and paint your front door red. Then return to the task at hand.

As you can tell, hiring then becomes the seventh step in a lengthy, involved process. If there is one decision a newly appointed principal needs to make cautiously, this is it. Like I wrote at the beginning of this chapter, your personnel will make or break you.

Sample interview questions: It is vital to construct and utilize valuable, meaningful questions for use in teacher interviews. The particular needs of each open position dictate the focus of the questions applied, so my advice is to be sure you know what you need and what you're looking for, then design or select questions that elicit appropriate responses. See appendix D for a sample interview form. That is by no means an exhaustive list, just a starting point. Talk to fellow administrators for their input in question design and the structure of an appropriate teacher interview.

Selecting the right people is, quite literally, your key to success. This is how you build your team. When you enter the fray, you will know what interpersonal dynamics are missing from this group equation, and with a diligent search you can uncover an individual that possesses those qualities. If your teaching staff is short on high-energy math experts and you have an opening, go get yourself a high-energy math expert. It's not rocket science, but it's important. Every opening is an opportunity, whether it is for a teacher, clinical aide, kitchen worker, teacher assistant, or half-time playground monitor/half-time attendance clerk. It is the door of possibility left ajar for you, the school, and the staff. Through personnel selection, a principal can influence climate, workplace morale, academic rigor, interpersonal relationships, discipline issues, and hordes of other aspects of the school environment.

Bob Talbert once said, "Good teachers are costly, but bad teachers cost more." Now I'll be honest with you: I don't know who the hell Bob Talbert is, but he obviously knew what he was talking about. Let me tell you a story:

Before the school year began, I was assembling my teaching staff. Because the former principal left to open a new school and subsequently took several staff members with her, I was forced to fill several openings, thirteen to be exact. One of these was a position that is particularly difficult to fill anyway, due to the stressful nature of the job duties. So I set out to fill the slot, but I did not follow the six-step process listed in this chapter. I did not actively recruit. I did not scour. I believe I included the right people and made the interview meaningful, but I did not scrutinize my top candidate thoroughly enough. I began to vacillate (this is not a medical term; don't worry, I'm perfectly healthy), and because we were less than a week from opening day, I pressed the accelerator and selected an unremarkable candidate. This person delivered a glowing interview that contrasted starkly with some glaring evaluations from a previous supervisor. But I felt painted into a corner with no other even remotely probable candidates, so I made the selection.

The time I spent over the next five months supervising this individual—by providing professional direction, arranging multiple means of assistance, recording a log of inappropriate actions, handling irate parents, fielding not-so-subtle accusations from the teachers' union, pacifying other staff members, and disciplining this individual—made me long for a time machine. What I would have given to go back and hire the right way! In retrospect, it would have been more beneficial to me, the school, and certainly those students to have begun the year with a substitute teacher until a qualified, permanent person made it through my checklist. The time, energy, heartache, and resolve it took to continue the process until this individual was ultimately reassigned to another site consumed significant portions of my days for weeks on end. And this did not allow me to perform the duties of educational leader for the other forty-nine members of the school staff. My parting words: Get it right the first time.

POINTS TO PONDER

- Personnel issues are the lifeblood of a principalship. To best hire, follow this six-step approach before hiring any personnel:
  - Actively recruit. Go find the good people.
  - Scour the applicant files. Search high and low for what the position needs.
  - Involve the right people. Assemble a strong interview team.
  - Make the interview matter. Ask questions that elicit the responses that inform you about the applicants.
  - Scrutinize the top candidate. Dig, ask, and find out. Take some time here.

- ○ Eliminate vacillation. Be sure. If you're not sure, don't offer the job.
- ○ Hiring the person is the seventh step in this process.
- Every opening is an opportunity. View it that way so that the opportunity is utilized most profitably for the entire school. Time spent in recruitment, selection, and careful hiring reduce the time spent remediating, assisting, and disciplining. Spend your time appropriately.

7

SUPERVISION AND EVALUATION

Leadership and learning are indispensable to each other.

—John F. Kennedy

In today's pluralistic school settings, the position of principal, with regards to the relationship between principal and teacher, has evolved cyclically over the decades, from facilitator to manager to supervisor and mentor. With the complicated reauthorization of the Elementary and Secondary Education Act (President Bush's "No Child Left Behind" legislation), there may be a push for the reemergence of the structured managerial method in the name of accountability, for the stakes have been unequivocally raised for all parties involved in the business of public education. Whatever the role you choose or are persuaded to take, I suggest you remember why you are in the business in the first place. Personally, I hope that you're here to make a difference in the world— one student, class, or school at a time. If so, keep that as your focus as you set forth on the process of supervising and evaluating your teachers. I am aware, and you should be, too, that almost half of your staff is formed by nonteaching personnel—counselors, custodians, secretaries, computer techs, teacher aides, kitchen staff, and so on. The strategies here can be used for those folks, too, though the primary emphasis throughout this chapter is handling and working with the teachers (that's why I keep writing *teachers* in this section—not because I'm ignoring the other staffers).

SUPERVISION

I'm going to make this as simple as I can, using short, one-syllable words so that everyone is sure to understand (or at least pronounce): If you want your folks to do the job and do it right, be there. There is no substitute for the presence of the principal, whether that means sitting in a classroom for an extended period of time, conducting formal five- to ten-minute walk-through observations in each classroom, entering the classroom from one door and proceeding directly to the other door, or even standing in the doorway or peering in the window as you walk by. Your presence matters.

A presenter at a conference I attended in Atlanta was the first to utter this quote within earshot of my radar: "Inspect what you expect." How true it rings, too. How often have you heard principals or other administrators curse the work ethics of their employees, groan at yet another incomprehensible blunder cast at the hands of their staff, bewail the tendencies of some folks to "coast" until formal evaluation time, or bemoan the fact that teacher X is always working on the computer and forwarding those damn chain e-mails during class? Well, what could one do about some of these dastardly scenarios? Take the following quick quiz, matching the options with the likely results:

Options	**Likely results**
A. Ignore them; they'll go away.	1. They'll go away all right: they'll balloon into unconquerable monsters.
B. Whine and moan, kick things, scream.	2. Raise your blood pressure, break your toe, develop laryngitis; the problems still exist.
C. Discipline the offenders right away.	3. Add the teachers' union to your list of problems.
D. Become a constant presence in and about their classrooms.	4. The troops straighten out.

Okay, so I made that quiz easy. A matches with 1, B with 2, C with 3, and D with 4. The point is simple: when the principal walks the grounds consistently, there is an unspoken understanding that everyone will be carrying out their duties with diligence and sufficient effort. The phenomenon is not unlike when you're driving that familiar stretch of road and you notice a police cruiser at the side of the road. Your foot explodes off the gas like a cat dropped in the bathtub. Even if you're traveling the speed limit (or slower), that's the instinct. But, on the grand scale, it's not law enforcement we as principals are after. Most teachers enjoy having the boss walk through the room: it helps straighten out the students, and it provides the teachers with a sense of security. *All is stable in the school; Principal Hall just dropped in, and José sure got on track when he came through. Ah, yes, now I can return to explaining the difference between a circle and a sphere for the seventh time. I love my job!* Knowing the cop is around just makes you feel better. (See appendix E for a quick walk-through sheet, which details how the principal can write quick notes to teachers—immediate written feedback can work wonders with your teachers.)

So how does a principal become a constant presence in the classrooms? First, you need to dedicate yourself to being an active, visible principal. Some things seem so simple but then become so difficult: *I have a grant proposal to finish! The guy is here about the broken window in room C-2! Dave in third grade just told Yasameen he was going to cut her hair with his shoelaces! I need to look up "wall-mounted TV/VCR stand" on the Internet so I can place that order today! I haven't written Mrs. Jesterton that letter of recommendation yet! The standardized tests have to be checked in! I'm swamped! I'll never leave the office!*

Well, guess what, Champ? Get your ass out of the office pronto! That work will still be there when you return, and your staff will be more efficient because of your active supervision. Prioritize your acts as principal, and if necessary, enroll yourself in a time management class. The choice is clear: Either spend more time in the building, in the classrooms, and in the hallways; or spend even more time mending the gaping wounds later. If you can, come to work early to get the paperwork done, answer e-mails, fill out forms, and write evaluations. Or stay late. Or delegate. (See appendix I for the bibliographic information on *The One-Minute Manager Meets the Monkey*, one of the greatest learn-to-delegate books of all time!) Or complete all that other stuff during the evening or the weekend—but don't spend your too much of your "away" time working. See chapter 11 for striking a balance between work and home.

Need a little nudge to get you out and moving around the building? Get a pedometer. Seriously. Ask for a donation from a sporting goods store, borrow one, buy one and write it off, whatever it takes. Just get one. Then start recording your distance traveled every day or during specific times of the day. When I started this practice, I was walking between two and four miles per day at school. Then it became a personal challenge, and I raised that to between three and five miles per day. Then I began passing it around the building. My head custodian (what a workaholic!) set the record with 9.3 miles in one day, but it's an interesting information-gathering tool, too. Give it to the teachers you sense are sitting a lot. Compare it with the ones you observe who are up and active. But more than anything: Get yourself up and active, then put the pedometer away!

The second part of effective supervision is addressing the individual needs of individual employees on an individual basis. We do not use the word *unique* to describe human beings just because there's no other cool word with a *q* in the middle. The word fits. And as a unique, special, diverse, distinct, idiosyncratic individual, each teacher requires and demands individual care. Now this takes some time, for it is not a simple undertaking to learn the nuances of fifty or more professionals on an individual basis in a plethora of combinations and contexts. So, if you did your homework as assigned in chapter 3 and you got to know the players, you're starting on the fifty-yard line.

Only through the course of the year, working day in and day out alongside these folks, will you truly acquire a sense for what makes each of them tick. Some teachers need a pat on the back every day. Some need public praising, others a quiet "thank you." Some need to be monitored more than an average bank teller. Some need friendly discourse, others stern interactions. Some need to be asked to participate on a committee; others need to be left alone. Some need written notes verifying their existence; some need to talk and be heard as often as possible. And it's not difficult to determine which individuals need which specific individual care—that is, if you, as principal, walk, observe, monitor, supervise, and listen—and to then provide that genuine individual service to keep the troops working at maximum efficiency with maximum rate of return.

Oh, and feed the teachers, will you? Publicly praise their efforts and their results. Invite them as a group to do something fun away from work—if the school budget has some money, take them to a nice lunch as a reward for nine weeks of hard work, for raising student literacy rates, for keeping the lunchroom clean, for not using all the allotted copy machine paper, whatever the reason. Make your e-mails personalized. It only takes a second or two to make note of something only you and Mr. Markusen know, but it lasts quite a while as Mr. Markusen reflects on his supervisor and how special he feels.

And this may sound terribly obvious, but smile as you greet each teacher every day. Your expressions of warmth are mighty statements to the value of your folks. Even if you're ticked off at so-and-so's parents, if the water main broke, if a substitute didn't show up, if your car has a flat tire, and if that little thread of carpet on your office floor gets stuck in the wheel of your chair and frays beyond repair, smile and say "Top of the morning, Mr. Griffith," then see if he knows the rest of that Irish expression and returns with, "And the rest of the day to you!" Let them know you care and recognize their work in the trenches.

EVALUATION

The way I see it, there are two types of evaluation in the school setting: formal, calendar evaluations; and informal, everyday evaluations. I made it very clear to my teaching staff that my position, as principal and manager of our site factory, quite literally involves the constant evaluation that accompanies all supervision and interaction that occurs in my presence. That means, simply, that I am always evaluating—that aspect of the position cannot be denied. That constant evaluation includes teachers, classroom setups, hallway conduct, student behavior, lunchroom decorations, telephone etiquette, parking alignment, copy machine care, prompt arrival of teachers at the conclusion of recess; you name it, I'm evaluating it.

The point of this introduction is not to make the staff nervous, nor is it to puff up your proverbial chest with some semblance of makeshift tangible authority. You're the principal; you have all the authority in the world in that school building. Encourage the staff, students, community, and visitors that we are constantly looking at improvement. No matter how good it is, there is always a way to make it better.

To provide a physical reminder of this philosophy, I got myself some personalized license plates that read 57GAMES. One of the "unbreakable" sports records is Joe DiMaggio's fifty-six-game hitting streak in 1941. Well, I believe there is a better player out there, waiting for the right conditions, attitude, and preparation to make a new record happen. To put it to a quick quote, "There is no ceiling atop your dreams."

As far as the formal evaluation process goes, this can be a tremendously helpful, productive system if implemented appropriately. A cynic might look at the teacher evaluation process and snicker, "Yeah, no one will ever read those formal written evaluations unless the teacher is failing, the principal is failing, the teacher is volunteering to transfer, or the file was accidentally placed in a folder labeled '101 Ways to Unjam a Copy Machine,' in the teacher's workroom." And that cynic may be right. However, that final written version of the evaluation is far, far less significant than the process by which the principal and teacher arrived at that point.

Formal evaluation of teaching staff is the most effective manner in which a principal can influence the educational process directly. The conversations between principal and teacher, oozing with specific suggestions, particular observations, and noteworthy reflections, are the key elements to productive, meaningful evaluation processes. The general steps are as follows:

1. Preevaluation conference. The principal and teacher meet to discuss the teacher's observation-and-evaluation schedule; to establish yearly goals (or quarterly, if that's more appropriate); and to contemplate any areas of emphasis for the district, school, grade level, or individual that year.

2. Formal observation periods. In a traditional sense, this includes the formal, established, scheduled, and discussed classroom observations of specific lessons. Lasting anywhere from thirty to ninety minutes, these observations provide a snapshot of the teacher's in-class performance. With the teacher's permission, these can be performed unscheduled, thereby illustrating a valid picture of the teaching and learning—that is, rather than the "dog and pony show" that the teacher has perfected by implementing it each of the last twenty-three consecutive years by bribing her students with chocolate and no-homework passes for good behavior and by asking intelligent-sounding questions while the principal is in the room.

3. Postobservation conferences. After each formal observation, the teacher and principal sit down and discuss the lesson, the implications of certain aspects of the lesson, and ramifications for future use. The teacher's reflections are paramount. I repeat: Let the teacher talk, wonder, and figure things out without too much "lecturing" from the principal. The principal is merely there to guide, probe, and question, providing input and observations as necessary.

4. Self-evaluation. As in each postobservation conference, the self-reflection and self-evaluation aspect is a powerful part of this process. Encourage the teachers to turn a critical eye on themselves and honestly assess their contributions to their students' learning. This can be quite an eye-opener for you, too, to determine if the teacher has a realistic self-image, is hypercritical, or even bothers to complete the form before the meeting.

Nowadays, most school districts have a specific protocol that principals follow to evaluate teachers, and it's usually a negotiated process made with the teachers' union. Don't deviate from that agreement without permission. But feel free to extend some liberties: provide a video camera so that the teacher can tape and later watch the lesson, joined only by self-consciousness, a half-empty bottle of sherry, and some grasshopper cookies; schedule more than the minimum number of formal observations, since that number really is a baseline amount; provide self-reflection forms for the teacher to complete after each lesson, to get the thoughts formalized (see appendix F); or do any other variation that you might find useful.

When dealing with individual teachers, remember their individual needs. To you, Mrs. Walstad may be just one of the thirty-two teachers you have to evaluate this year; but to Mrs. Walstad, she is one of one. Treat her that way, and remember that the foundation of the evaluation process is continuous, consistent improvement. A statement I make to teachers at one point or another (or repeatedly throughout the series; sometimes I forget who has already heard it) is "I'm here to help you deliver instruction better (or manage transitions better, or provide feedback to students more effectively, . . .). If there is anything I can provide to help you improve your professional practice, I will offer it. If there is anything you would like from me during this process, please tell me. In the end, I'm here to help you. Our common goal is to provide the best possible educational experience for the students with whom you interact, so that's what we'll do." Once the table is set, you can serve almost any meal in the name of improvement and support.

SUPPORT

Support. There's a term you'll use. The responsibility of the principal is to provide meaningful support to the teachers. To do so properly, the principal must know what kind of support each teacher needs. Refer to the teacher's established annual goals, utilize any notes you have compiled regarding that individual, and consult personally with the teacher often. When delivering feedback—whether positive or negative, whether it is in person or in writing—be specific. Generalizations mean nothing, but clear, precise feedback with matching suggestions or questions are useful and appreciated. Plus, specifics give you a focal point during your next walk-through or formal observation.

If the conversation turns to an area with which the teacher needs strengthening or improvement, don't leave it with that statement. The type of comment that will simply irk the teacher and restrict your impact later is, for example, "You need to do a better job of arranging the furniture in your room. It's too cluttered." Find a teacher within the building with better furniture arrangement; agree to cover the spatially challenged teacher's classroom for a half hour one day, and allow that teacher to observe the organized teacher's pristine room setup. In short, have a practical suggestion and a resource available prior to leveling any sort of criticism, constructive or otherwise. That's the type of meaningful, individual support and assistance the job requires and the teachers deserve.

If you are going to schedule a formal observation with a teacher, stick to it. The teacher expects you to be there, and your prompt arrival signifies a respect that is difficult to earn back if you're a no-show. Be there, and be on time. Every time.

For the most part, teachers work as hard as they know how to work. They do the best job they have the training and skills to do. For the majority of your teaching staff, that will be sufficient. There are generally three levels of teachers on-site, grouped as follows:

Thoroughbreds (about 20 percent of the staff). These folks are the first to arrive, the last to leave, and are the hardest-working individuals in between. They will do whatever you ask, cheerfully and with great enthusiasm. They often volunteer for more. They tutor at recess; they make extra phone calls home; they discuss education with their colleagues; and they get the job done well. These are the folks whom you build a staff around, whom you seek out for advice, and whom you listen to—because when they speak, it's gospel.

Middle-of-the-packers (about 65 percent of the staff). These folks, the MOPs, get the job done, but they need a certain degree of direct supervision and external motivation. They may lack some of the *Go-get-'em* mentality that separates the thoroughbreds from the rest. With appropriate support, pressure, empowerment, and cajoling, these folks do what is asked of them.

Lollygaggers (about 15 percent of the staff). Someone once told me, "Spend 85 percent of your time and energy with the 85 percent of your staff that will follow you." If my math is correct, that leaves just 15 percent of my time for the heel-dragging lollygaggers. That 15 percent is characterized by either an unwillingness to follow contract hours (i.e., frequent late arrivals) or an excessive demand to follow contract hours (i.e., gone the instant the contract hours are up). They're not interested in receiving training; they express sullen or surly attitudes; they lead the charge in the parking-lot moaning sessions; and some don't even seem to like children. For them, change is not only scary, but it is unacceptable. For the sake of the rest of this section, we'll refer to those teachers as the ACI folks, because they *ain't cuttin' it*.

The first rule for handling an ACI is to treat, support, and offer guidance to that individual just as you would with any other member of the staff. Fairness and consistency are the ballasts that keep your leadership on an even keel, and word travels fast whether a principal is unjustly picking on a teacher or genuinely holding that ACI to the same standard as everyone else. You'd like to stick with the latter rather than the former. A little-acknowledged truth about the ACI population is that it comprises two subgroups: MCIWSI and ANGCI. The MCIWSI necessitate a good deal of your positive energy because they *might cut it with serious intervention.* The ANGCI, however, will test your intestinal fortitude, for they *ain't never gonna cut it,* and you can spot these folks in a crowd quicker than a giraffe in a well-lit bowling alley.

Remember in chapter 5 how we talked about picking your battles and weighing the cost versus the benefits of each situation you'll face? Well, when you're facing questions of employee competence and the employee in question is charged with the education of young children for 180 days of their lives, it's not as simple as you may think. Not every poor teacher can be trained to an acceptable level of mediocrity, but not every poor teacher can be eliminated, either. Remember the mantra: Always strive to be a better you. *E pluribus unum.* Make the decision based on what is best for the students and the school as a whole. If stripping your time, energy, and positive attitude is not best for the school, even if ridding the site of that poor teacher is, you may have to bite the bullet and ride out the storm. It's hard to give a subpar worker par ratings, but sometimes that's the only path realistically available. And if you're going to take the road that leads to employee dismissal, be sure— collect the data, prepare for the attackers, take time for on-site damage control, seek counsel from your superiors at the district office, and stay the course. Don't stop fighting until the fighting's through. But you better be sure.

Here is a tale from the trenches that I just couldn't wait until chapter 10 to share. As a first-year principal, I was as fearless as Indiana Jones when he faced the sword-wielding duo on the cliffs above the river . . . until he realized he had no pistol. Here's the tale.

I had erroneously hired a teacher whose skills were absent and whose ability to motivate children ran parallel to your garden-variety CPA. My fault for not following the six-step process, I know. That's twice, if you're counting at home. Regardless, I held true to my integrity and awarded this teacher an "Unsatisfactory" during the December evaluation period, the first of three grading sessions. I gave specific feedback, and I explained what I wished to see. I set up this individual with peers and quality folks at other school sites for observations. I provided support. This teacher received a second "Unsatisfactory" during the February evaluation. At this time, I created a site-based, individualized direct assistance plan (DAP) for this teacher. The DAP provided the necessary evidence, according to NEAT (notice, expectations, assistance, timeline), to proceed with dismissal if I didn't see improvement over the next two months. This individual, by the way, was a no-holds-barred ANGCI.

When I was preparing to scribe the third and final "Unsatisfactory," I consulted with the folks in the human resources department, who told me that I could not recommend nonrenewal of this teacher's contract because we did not send her a notice of possible nonrenewal by the deadline, which was one month prior. However, with three "Unsatisfactory" evaluations, a teacher could not be recommended for tenured status, either.

So what does a new principal do? I sought guidance from HR and from my direct supervisor. Clearly, the ANGCI was not good for the profession or for the children. However, equally clear was the legal stand that the teachers' union would take, and rightly so, in that I did not follow procedure by providing written notification of the possible nonrenewal. I would lose that battle in arbitration, so I was advised to drop it, concede, swallow my integrity, write the evaluation as "Satisfactory," and recommend the teacher for full tenure. So I did. And it burns me still.

The lesson I learned from this is twofold: first, go back and hire properly, nitwit; second, find out the procedures and timelines in your school district for dismissing an ineffective or harmful teacher. Know the path before traveling it—which is the same thought process that directed me to write this book, not incidentally.

POINTS TO PONDER

- If you are going to supervise your troops, supervise them. Be there. Walk through the classrooms, observe the teachers, supervise the lunchroom, attend training sessions, go where the action is. If you want quality workers to do quality work, "inspect what you expect."
- Get out of the office during the school day. The paperwork, e-mails, and phone calls will still be there when you return, and the benefits of your consistent presence will be felt continuously.
- Assess and address the individual needs of each individual employee on an individual basis. Feed the hungry, empower the meek, lift the downtrodden, free the spirited.

- There are two types of evaluations: formal, calendar evaluations; and informal, everyday evaluations. As principal, you cannot avoid evaluating all interactions and situations constantly; it's part of the job. Let your staff know that reality.
- The formal evaluation process can be quite useful in improving instruction. Maintain the goal of assisting teachers as they strive to master their craft—focus on continuous, consistent improvement.
- When providing criticisms (constructive or otherwise), be specific. Precise feedback with practical suggestions are meaningful to the teachers and demonstrate your willingness to assist them in their improvement.
- Know the staff: you have three classes of personnel:
  - *Thoroughbreds* (20 percent). They will run and run to better themselves and to provide superb services to students.
  - *MOPs* (65 percent). These middle-of-the-packers get the job done with proper support and encouragement.
  - *ACIs* (15 percent). These folks ain't cuttin' it. They need a lot of work, but not at the expense of the other 85 percent. Support them as you would support any other teacher. Maintain fairness and consistency.

8

THE THREE GOLDEN RULES

If people knew how hard I worked to achieve my mastery, it wouldn't seem so wonderful after all.

—Michelangelo

If you only read one chapter of this book, make it this one.

In the first several months of the job, I put together a rather simple formula for experiencing success with regards to students, parents, teachers, the school site, achievement, budgets, parking, substitutes, class assignments, supplies, books, procedures, schedules, ideas, hairdos, foot attire, and cleavage. It involves three basic ideas that I refer to as the three golden rules. This is not "Do unto others as you would have done unto you," for that is the capitalized Golden Rule, to which we all ought to strive in our multifaceted lives. No, these three golden rules are specifically for a new principal. In no particular order, but in perfect honesty, here they are, as I know them:

- Stay true to the shared vision.
- Be aware of the goings-on.
- Conduct yourself professionally.

Stay true to the shared vision. Align every decision, every expenditure, every comment, and every request with the common goal as agreed upon by your teaching staff and site personnel. With this as the driving force behind all decision-making processes and as the justification for all directions, nobody can refute your intentions or question your integrity. This is not to say that nobody can question your ideas or your rationality, but your motives are beyond reproach when you explain, "We have chosen this path because it is clearly in the best interest of our students, and this is why . . ." Even when individuals, or even groups, disagree with your decisions, they will not knock your motivation if you are precise with your explanation and provide adequate data or reasoning to support your cause.

As principal, you have to make what seems like hundreds of thousands of decisions, maybe more. Some are easy; others are substantially more difficult (see chapter 5 for information on picking your battles). When those difficult decisions arise, decline the temptations to cast your wand whimsically. Listen to, but do not base decisions on, the pleas of individuals who have some personal interest in the outcome of any single situation. The single, solitary, lone, sole, only, primary focal point should be the common goal. Ask yourself, and anyone else involved in the decision-making process, "Is this aligned with our vision of the school as a whole?" If the justification is there, honest and real, then proceed with your decision. If nothing else, doing so provides you with clear direction.

I wrote the words *E pluribus unum* on the whiteboard in my office, in plain view of anyone that entered or even stood in the main office near my door. This Latin phrase, known popularly as the motto of the United States, means "Out of many, one." For my school setting, I interpret this phrase as such: We have five hundred students, each with individual skills, habits, hopes, and dreams. The same can be said for our fifty staff members, innumerable community dwellers, and the multitudes that interact with our students and staff on a daily basis. We cannot possibly please each and every one of them, satisfying each individual's individual needs with precise individual care. What we can do is this: we can join together with a common goal, striving together toward a clear and agreed-on vision, and we can forego some of the individual desires for the good of the whole. Out of many, we have one goal. *E pluribus unum.*

That Latin phrase, written on the office wall, serves as a physical reminder that every decision I make—while sitting in that principal's chair and operating on behalf of the staff, students, and school community—must be aligned with our vision. If I cannot say that it is, unequivocally and without hesitation, I must not make that decision.

Some questions and issues—such as "Do we have funds to reimburse the soccer coach for the four pizzas he bought for the team after last week's game?"—do not really affect the long-term attainment of the vision. Others—such as "Should we use that last allocation as a fifth-grade classroom teacher or as an upper-grade remedial reading teacher?" or "During our literacy block, should we group students by ability level or grade level?"—can have a profound impact on the path traveled by all. These are the types of questions to which I refer, where a whimsical decision can be devastating. Instead of deciding capriciously, do the research, question the parties involved, determine the pros and cons, analyze the cost and benefits, reflect on any input, consult the folks in your inner circle, and critically compare your proposed decision with your school's accepted goals.

Be aware of the goings-on. In regards to every aspect of your school premises—know what is happening, how it is happening, why it is happening, where it is happening, when it is happening, and to whom or with whom it is happening. Use your eyes and ears for their intended purposes: observe and listen, constantly and consistently. You have no excuse for being surprised when a parent calls to complain of a repeated problem with her child's teacher. There is no reason for a teacher to come to you, exasperated, and lament, "This is enough. That teacher assistant is never in the class she's assigned. She reeks of smoke, and she's always late." It would be incomprehensible for you to not be aware of the problem before a duty teacher asks, "What are we going to do about the kids kicking the balls over the fence and then hopping over to get them? It happens about fifteen times per recess."

It is your job to know what is going on. It is your responsibility to know the teaching styles of each individual under your supervision. It is your obligation to know the general behavior of your students in comparison with the established rules of conduct within and outside the classrooms. It is your duty to know where the classes are during each period, each day of the week. It is your function to know the relationships between colleagues and all the nuances of interpersonal communication within your school building. It is your job to know what is going on.

The best way to acquire this knowledge is to engage those two critical senses, seeing and hearing, throughout the day, every day. I once met with a superintendent in Kennewick, Washington, who told me of a "two–ten promise," which every administrator in his school district had made: they pledged to be in the classrooms of their schools for two hours every day, or ten hours every week. This forced them to hold to what they should have been doing all along anyway: observing and listening. Active supervision. Monitor and manage. Walk the beat. Conduct walk-throughs. Whatever term fits your understanding, use it to your advantage.

Just be sure to spend the time within your building actively, listening to the students, observing the teachers, noting patterns, providing visibility, answering questions, alleviating concerns, and collecting valuable qualitative data to file in your gray matter database. The mileage you put on your Asics lace-ups, as reflected on your hip pedometer (see chapter 7), pay monstrous dividends when you address the needs of your staff and school community.

Think of it this way: If you do not know what is going on in your own building, then how can you direct it toward the shared vision?

Conduct yourself professionally. During interactions with your clients, comrades, or competitors, remember that you are the figurehead of your school organization. Be the professional leader. Schools and education in general get a bad rap for being a blue-collar psuedo-profession. Mark my words: Teaching is a profession, and all those intertwined with the direct instruction of our nation's future are professionals. You, as principal, are the chief pro of the group.

As I mentioned earlier, at times it is difficult to separate your emotions from your professional responsibilities. It is hard to maintain a cool, calm, and collected approach in the face of absurdity. It is tough to stay detached, wiping away your personal wishes and making a decision based on what is best for the whole, rather than what is easiest for you or someone on your staff. This job tries your patience; it strings you up at your wits' end; it tongue-ties you with mounds of irrelevant nonsense; it shackles you with regulations; and it frustrates you beyond measure, with arguments, confrontation, and complaints that needn't exist. In each of these situations, your responses as the chief pro dictate the environment, atmosphere, and overriding attitude of your staff and those within your scope.

There are a couple of ways that you can maintain a professional edge when dealing with the neurotic, erratic, volatile, frustrated, emotional, and just plain loony. These also work with the normal, friendly, typical, fun, and balanced. In fact, they should guide most of your interpersonal interactions while on the job:

Be pleasant. This goes without saying, but I'll say it anyway. Your demeanor plays a giant role in interpersonal communications. In addition to the actual words you say and the tone with which you say them, this has to do with facial expressions and body language, for research indicates as much as 90 percent of your message is portrayed through nonverbal cues. Just be nice. Give the person your time and energy; smile; ask about the family; discuss the concern, question, or request with polite dialogue. No matter what your response or decision is, propose it with genuine respect for the audience, for their reception of the information sometimes carries as much weight as the information itself.

Maintain focus. Keep the conversation focused. If you sense it starting to drift, redirect it. If you sense yourself starting to drift, redirect yourself. In the principalship, most of your interpersonal interactions are resolution based. That is to say, people come to you with questions they want answered, concerns they want addressed, requests they want approved, or complaints of situations they want rectified. Your accepted duty, typically, is to resolve those issues, one way or another. It compounds your problem when you tackle more than you can handle in one conversation, so it behooves you to maintain that focus on one issue at a time. If a person comes to you with one problem and it starts to multiply like rabbits, call time-out and ask that person to bring any additional concerns to you at a later time; for now, you must focus on first things first.

Listen. This is the number-one rule of all communication. In a leadership position, you could go around telling everyone everything all the time, but soon you would have disenchanted those under your charge. Instead, listen. Hear what the concern is; understand the other person's point of view; discern if there is an underlying problem manifesting itself in a surface problem; and engage in active listening. Ask questions. Paraphrase. Request clarification. You cannot possibly help a person resolve a conflict or answer a question if you do not have a firm understanding of the dispute or query to begin with.

Let it go. Sometimes, you find yourself dealing with an irrational mind (hopefully, not your own). This may come from any direction at any time, and it may frustrate you, irritate you, anger you, mystify you, befuddle you, or exasperate you for a variety of reasons. In these cases, maintaining your calm is crucial. Simply listen to the ranting, thank the individual for any input or suggestions, and excuse yourself from the conversation. Later, when you're reflecting on your day and you think of this exchange, consider the source, smile, and take your dog for a nice walk.

Be neutral. One of the more difficult things for new principals to do is to step back from the "part of the gang" mentality and establish consistent, equal relationships among the staffers in the building. Naturally, you will be drawn toward certain individuals: some will have common interests with you; some will have personalities that mesh with yours; and some you will simply get to know better for whatever reason, say, as a result of working on a project together or perhaps simply sharing proximity. This is fact. However, it is also a fact that everyone in the school will know if Mrs. Snyder got the big classroom because she's the "principal's pet." Nothing erodes the morale of a staff quicker than the feeling that the boss is playing favorites. If you deny a request to a teacher, make it for the right reasons and be prepared to deny that request to any or all of the teachers, should they too make that request. I caution you against socializing with individual members of the teaching staff for precisely that reason, to avoid favoritism. Your professionalism is at stake here, and with such importance, your interactions with all staffers should remain firmly neutral.

There you have them: the three golden rules. If you follow these principles, you should not have any surprise attacks that catch you defenseless. With such a tremendous opportunity to make a difference in the world, don't you suppose the least you could do is maintain the professional edge? After all, you're the chief pro . . .

POINTS TO PONDER

- The principalship is a difficult, demanding job. To keep your head above water throughout that first year, I recommend that you follow the three golden rules:
  1. *Stay true to the shared vision.* Align all decisions and spending with the common goals, as established by the school community.

Ask yourself before any decision, "Is this aligned with our vision of the school as a whole?" Remember the meaning of *E pluribus unum*. If it helps, write this where you will see it every day.

2. Be aware of the goings-on. It is your job to know what is going on in your school. Listen and observe throughout the day, every day. Make a two–ten promise to yourself and your staff. Be there. If you don't know what's going on in your building, how can you direct it toward the shared vision?

3. Be professional. As Theodore Roosevelt said, "The most important single ingredient in the formula of success is knowing how to get along with people." Be pleasant, maintain your focus, listen, be neutral, and stay emotionally detached. It is a job; remember that. Conduct yourself professionally.

CATCH-ALL

The price of greatness is responsibility.

—Sir Winston Churchill

A person needs to know so many things before tackling the behemoth principalship that this book could probably go on forever detailing them. However, you have a job to do, and, quite frankly, so do I. So, this "meaty" chapter is meant to pull in several of the outliers, with the intended purpose of helping the rookie principal understand a couple more of the peculiarities of the position.

SUPERVISING/DISCIPLINING CHILDREN

Quite plainly, children are the reason we have a job. Without children, there is no school; and without a school, you sure as heck aren't going to be a principal of one. So it follows that children should be the focal point of your business as chief pro of the school. I have written about making decisions based on the best interests of the children and on keeping the good of the whole as the driving force of conversations. But what about when school begins, and there are children in the building?

Supervise them. Just as teachers and other staff members need and appreciate your active supervision, so do children. They, too, wish to know their limits, and they need your proactive management. I have seen the other side, at schools in which the principal does not actively supervise the students, and those principals are the ones that complain about all the discipline they have to do, about the teachers who cannot handle the students, about the children who are rowdy and out of control . . . why would you want that for yourself? Honor that two–ten pledge (see chapter 8) by walking through classrooms but also spend a significant amount of time among the students outside of class—on the playground during recess, in the lunchroom during lunch, and in the hallways during transitions.

I make a concerted effort to be active and visible before school: I am on the playground during every recess period; I monitor the lunchroom during the noon hour; and I supervise the crossing guards down the street after school. The students see me. I see them. We have an understanding regarding behavioral expectations, and because of my presence, I can settle disputes before they become fights or serious problems. I call this "proactive discipline."

Personally, I enjoy my time outside, and I do it as often as I can. Walking the grounds during recess is one of the job perks—fresh air, children laughing, students constantly running up to deliver high fives . . . these are the immediate rewards of the principalship that you rarely hear about. By being where the students are, you have the opportunity to gain their trust, to establish yourself as a constant presence, to build relationships, to assure the masses that there is control, and to solve problems early. As a result of this effort, when a student does get in trouble, being sent to the principal's office is not a frightening experience because it involves the unknown; rather, it is a nerve-wracking time because the student knows he or she has messed up and has let down someone who cares. When you build firm relationships with students, your leverage is scores more powerful when handling discipline referrals.

When it comes to the act of disciplining students, I follow the creed "Discipline with dignity." The point is teaching, or training, the students to use appropriate behavior. You must maintain respect to continue in that direction. Further, I believe every child, as an individual, deserves individual consideration and specific care. A chronic offender who steals five dollars from a teacher's purse might not necessarily receive the same consequence as a first-time offender, depending on the situation. The punishment must fit the crime, but it also must fit the child who broke the rule. I typically assign every child that is sent to the office some of the same consequences: each child must phone his or her own parents and relay the message, and each child must somehow atone for his or her misdeed. Beyond those, the consequences vary from situation to situation and from child to child.

When I arrived at my new school, there was an established multiple-step discipline procession with matching citation forms, charts, and assigned consequences. I have enough faith in my own ability to learn about my students and then "learn 'em" in appropriate behaviors—through modeling, instruction, discipline, and consequences—that I eliminated that procession. I don't advocate that you do that as a new principal until you are sure of yourself in the supervision/discipline arena, but it has worked for me so far. Discipline referrals are way down over last year, and there is a feeling of peace on the playground and around the campus.

HANDLING DIFFICULT PARENTS

One aspect of the job that is never addressed in administrative coursework or preservice programs regards handling the "parent from hell." In chapter 8, I share with you the three golden rules, one of which included several steps to maintaining professionalism even in the face of absurdity, and here is where those steps will come into play.

There will be parents who want their child moved out of a class for a variety of interesting reasons (there's a bully in the room; the teacher is mean; the work is too easy; the classroom is on the west side of the building, and Johnny can't be exposed to afternoon sunlight); they want the teacher's head on a platter because she wouldn't let their child go to the bathroom one day; they insist they did not receive the notice about the science fair and want heads to roll as a result; they want to know why the school is picking on their child; they want to borrow thirty dollars for a bus ticket to go pick up their laundry from a town 140 miles away; they want to know why the school doesn't focus on social studies like it used to . . . you name it, they've requested it. However, you must listen to each request, regardless of how ludicrous it is. That simply comes with the territory.

Your demeanor plays a big role in the direction of the conversation, so you should be keenly aware of your response. Some parents come in hotheaded and volatile, looking for blood. I have found that the best re-action is to generally remain calm and not give in to the urge to puff up my chest and take 'em on. For me, being peaceful and soothing, allow-ing the person to vent, has worked more often than not. I cannot even count the number of times parents came in breathing fire, vowing to call the school board or the superintendent, telling me "something better be done about this." I just sit and listen and have since developed a knack for looking quizzically and asking, "Are you threatening me? That sounds like a threat. Is that how we are going to solve this problem?" As I wrote in the previous chapter, maintain your professionalism, focus on the problem, and stay emotionally detached. In short, be cool. I have had parents enter my office screaming at me, then leave my office want-ing to hug me. Don't take any of it personally—parents are generally up-set at the situation, even though they take it out on the people (you).

I don't remember where this story came from, but I heard the tale of a rather resilient principal who was working late in his office one evening. A parent came in and stood in the doorway. The principal did not look up, just told the visitor, "Do you have an appointment to see me?" The visitor said he did not but pulled out a pistol and pointed it at the principal. At this point the principal looked up, sighed, and stated, "I'm sorry, but if you don't have an appointment I cannot meet with you. You'll have to come back tomorrow." The shocked parent put away the gun and walked out, muttering. Now that's cool and detached.

PR IN THE COMMUNITY

Schools get a bad rap these days, especially public schools. And if you are assigned a needy, low-achieving school in a high-poverty neighbor-hood as I was (and let's face it, most new principals are; that's how the system is set up), your school probably does not get much positive attention at all. It's important for the morale of the staff, students, and school community that all of the good things occurring in your school is shared throughout the community, through the newspaper and neighborhood publicity.

The local newspaper can be your friend, or it can be a vial of toxic waste. If your school is a Title I school, you receive extra federal funding to offset the high-poverty neighborhood economics, but you should brace yourself for the onslaught of regulations and sanctions if the student achievement does not grow in accordance with federal guidelines. And believe me, the newspaper learns of these (both the low achievement and the sanctions), and they have fun with them. If this happens, the folks living in your neighborhood will question the quality of the education their children are receiving. This is a proverbial can of worms.

I recommend taking a business approach by making a public relations pitch, however grassroots or elemental it may seem. Here are some ideas for spreading the good word.

Make a school brochure. Share the site statistics, demographics, and program narratives, delivered in a handy format with photos and contact information. Keep copies handy in the office and share them with parents, other administrators, the cashier at the neighborhood deli, anyone within reach.

Call the local education reporter and invite that person to the building. Share the positive data; ask that person to bask in the warmth of the atmosphere; and give the reporter some specific, tangible proof that the school is all right. Hand out a brochure, too, and give one to the camera guy.

Create a school website. Link information about the teachers, the mascot, the school building, and the educational program. Recruit the technologically savvy to assist in its maintenance.

Beautify the school itself. Paint the spots that need painting. Plant new trees. Erect a signboard with upcoming events. Get new carpeting. All of these cost money, but they are worth it to prove that you value the building in which five hundred children spend several hours per day.

Be visible in the community. Attend neighborhood advisory board meetings, shop in the local markets. Let people know you are the principal of the most wonderful school in the district and that you are proud to be there. At school district functions, comment on the strengths of your staff, the terrific students, and the supportive parents. The word will spread.

Join a service organization. There are plenty to choose from in most areas: Lions, Rotary, Moose, Elk, Platypus . . . whatever fits your fancy. These are tremendous avenues to meet people, to network, and to provide an audience for you to sing the praises of your staff, students, neighborhood, parents, and educational program.

BUDGET ISSUES: PRIORITIZING AND SPENDING

As I wrote in the previous section, if you are placed in a Title I school, you have a substantial amount of funding to supplement your meager general-fund budget. If you are clever at writing grants, you could acquire for the school additional funds to assist the programs. But money, needless to say, is not the answer. Spending money wisely can, however, be a tremendous asset.

If you are like me, this is probably your first real experience in charge of a significant amount of money, an amount tied closely with public accountability and designated solely for the purpose of better educating children. Through grants, Title I funds, and the general budget, we had accounts totaling over a quarter of a million dollars, all for the purpose of running a school. Granted, most of that money goes directly to auxiliary personnel, such as teacher assistants, literacy coordinators, and parent involvement facilitators; but there was still a large stack under the mattress left for materials, supplies, professional development, technology, and other categories not so specific. How do you spend that other chunk of change?

First of all, turn immediately back to chapter 8 and reread the first of the three golden rules: "Stay true to the shared vision." If allocating the money on project Z does not further the shared vision, then don't spend it on project Z. It's that simple. And if you're planning on allocating $150 on project Z for teacher A, you'd better allocate $150 to teachers B through X as well. That's just a survival tip.

Next, evaluate your school's current situation in relation to the path toward the common goal. List and prioritize the steps, materials, and goods necessary to propel you down that correct path. Just as in any other decision, weigh the pros and cons, measure the costs and benefits, deliberate the likely outcomes, and determine whether the expenditure meets your criteria. Consult the folks in your inner circle if you have any hesitation. You want to be especially certain before spending any large sums of money that your budget statements, when they become public knowledge, are defensible under the umbrella of "in the best interest of our students, in order to improve their educational experience in the following manner . . ."

FINISHING THE YEAR

As the school year wraps up and you begin to file everything into your "first-year principal" file (which, I hope, is not your office recycle bin), postpone counting the remaining days—you still have work to do. You can ask your spouse, your supervisor, your parakeet, or your secretary how effective your initial year in the job was, but it's unlikely you'll get an untainted version of the truth. You need to get your input straight from the proverbial horse's mouth: the teachers themselves. But how do you get honest, real feedback about the boss from the employees? I advocate a simple method: ask them.

Now, you have probably established yourself as the type of leader that is interested in student achievement, excellence, professional growth, and anything that is in the best interest of the collective whole. Certainly you have proven your integrity, so now it's time to demonstrate your humility. Ask your teachers how the school year went. Ask them about your rookie year. Ask them to give you their appraisal of your leadership skills, strategies, and methods. I have included as appendix H a sample questionnaire of sorts that provides a format for this input. To avoid the temptation to become an amateur handwriting analyst to figure out who wrote what, ask a trusted friend to type the teachers' responses.

When I did this at the conclusion of my first year, I piggybacked it with the second installment of the belief system questionnaire (see appendix G), to get a feel for the staff's attitudes and beliefs and to determine whether they had shifted their opinions over the course of the year. The results, if authentic, are quite informative and very interesting to read. Remember to keep a thick skin—if the teachers were as honest as you asked them to be, you will learn some things about yourself you may never have imagined.

POINTS TO PONDER

- When it comes to supervising children, supervise them. Be there. Be a visible presence: this is called "proactive discipline," and it saves you oodles of time later.
- Discipline students with dignity. Remember: the child is good, even if the behavior is bad. If you have built solid relationships with students, by being visible and present, you will have more leverage with direct discipline. You are to train appropriate behaviors, not nail students for messing up.
- Your demeanor is crucial in handling erratic parents. Do not take their ranting tirades personally—people get upset at the situation, even though the person (you) will have to take the brunt of it.
- Increase the positive image of your school throughout the community. Build a strong foundation of your site's excellence by engaging in the following:
  - Make a school brochure.
  - Call the local education reporter.
  - Create a school website.
  - Beautify the school campus.
  - Be visible in the community.
  - Join a service organization.
- Budget concerns are valid and confounding. Prioritize the school's needs and ensure that the expenditure is aligned with the school's common vision. Spending money wisely can be a tremendous asset, but spending frivolously opens new cans of worms.
- Finish the year by requesting honest feedback from your teachers. It helps.

⑩

TALES OF COMBAT

"I'm your huckleberry."

—Val Kilmer, playing Wyatt Earp's buddy Doc Holliday in
Tombstone

Sometimes, it's just a fight. Depending on the scenario, it may be a fight to the teeth; it may be a fight to survive; it may be a fight based on principle; it may be a fight for pride; it may really be a fight worth fighting; it may even be a fight to keep from laughing.

The following are all true stories, meant to lighten your mood as you approach the prospect of a principalship. You may interpret each one however it suits you. My writing may provide a slant toward humor, aggression, or even frustration, but don't let that sway your own perceptions. Use these anecdotes for therapy, brainstorming, empathy, or enlightenment. And, if I may be so bold, I suggest that you record your own tales from the trenches, publish them, and retire off the royalties. But send me a check for one hundred dollars because it was my idea.

MUSIC VERSUS MEDITATION

At my school, we have a designated all-school literacy block, during which every child in the school (grades one through six) is regrouped for reading instruction, according to ability. This means that the students must change classrooms. To facilitate this transition—which could be chaotic, with over four hundred six to twelve year olds moving from classroom to classroom at the same time—we play music over our PA system. Frequently, the music consists of upbeat oldies, such as Creedence or the Oak Ridge Boys, or something fun and high paced. This energizes the students, prepares the teachers, and is a clear indication of the transition period (which only lasts two minutes). When the music starts, the students set off for their reading class; when it ends, they'd better be there or they are marked tardy.

Since we have portable classrooms that are not connected to the main building and students have to walk through a courtyard during this passing time, I elected to utilize our outside speakers for our daily dance party so that those students could enjoy the music and time their travel as well.

One morning, three days into the new school year, we got a phone call from a neighborhood resident. "Turn off that music," she screamed to me. "It's interrupting my yoga time. How can I meditate with all that rap music?"

"Ma'am," I replied. "I hardly consider Bob Dylan to be rap music. Is there any way you could reschedule your yoga time? We play our music from 9:03 to 9:05 every morning. You can bank on it. How about you start yoga at 9:06?"

After a call from the superintendent, we decided that this was one battle a third-day principal did not need to fight. I turned off the outside speakers.

PAIN VERSUS SUICIDE

Early in the school year, one of the socially challenged students in our self-contained behavior-modification class was causing a ruckus in the classroom and fled to the steps just outside the door. She then climbed the railing and stood, screaming at the top of her lungs that she was going to jump.

My dean of students, a clever future principal himself, walked down to the portable building and walked up the five steps to where the girl was perched atop the railing. After he asked her what she was doing up there, she told him, "I'm going to jump and kill myself."

The dean looked at the girl, then looked down to the blacktop, just eight feet below. As his gaze met hers again, he shook his head solemnly. "Oh, I don't think so," he sighed. "From that height, you won't kill yourself. You'll get hurt, though. When you hit that blacktop, a couple of the bones in your legs will break, and maybe your wrists will, too. The jagged edges will be sticking out through your skin, and the blood will get all over your clothes. You'll be in a lot of pain, that's for sure."

She stepped down and walked back inside quietly, without incident.

BEWARE THE OVERAGE, MY SON

In my school district, after the voluntary transfer period is completed, the district reserves the right to place teachers in schools through a directed transfer period. This happens if a position is eliminated, if a school is overallocated, or if a personnel issue needs to be resolved, resulting in an individual's needing an alternate placement. The district does its best to fit skills with needs, but sometimes it just doesn't work that way.

Six weeks into my first year, we were forced to "overage" three teachers, due to our lower-than-expected student enrollment (to "overage" a teacher is a euphemistic way of saying "you're outta here . . . and into a different school"). One resigned, so that was an easy solution. One teacher, who had been directly transferred to my school in the first place, volunteered to be overaged again, thus escaping what was to be a tumultuous year working for me. That left one.

When nobody else volunteers, our district's procedure is to select the teacher with the shortest district tenure to place on the overage list. We had three teachers with the same hire date, so we went to plan B. In Reno, especially at a school whose mascot name is the Aces, what could be more apropos than drawing cards to determine who stays and who leaves? I can't believe that the negotiations between district and union folks have not resulted in a better resolution than "high card stays," but that's life in Reno. By the way, if and when you conduct this practice, always have the union's building rep present in the room.

Each of the players took a card, and the teacher with the low card was selected by default for the overage list. This is an emotional experience not to be taken lightly. Even if the principal has a teacher that is clearly better for the students (or vice versa), it's not appropriate to shout, "Aw, shoot, I thought that queen was high enough!" or "Yes! You won, way to go! Thank God." Draw, record, hug, and let them cry or cheer elsewhere.

MISS NEVADA

One lucky day in the spring of my inaugural year, we were graced with the appearance of our very own Miss Nevada, Teresa Benitez. She was on her tour of schools, offering presentations to groups of students and sharing the wisdom of staying in school and of the power of positive thinking. We scheduled her to sit and conduct a "fireside chat" (sans fire, of course) with our sixth-grade girls, while we sent the boys outside to play kickball or do something masculine so that they wouldn't drool and slobber and ruin the presentation.

As our dean of students walked Miss Benitez to the classroom where she would meet our sixth-graders, a very expressive third-grade boy walked past them and did a double take. He stopped and watched this gorgeous young lady walk by and, in a very teenageresque move, visually checked her out as she passed.

Our dean noticed this and likewise stopped. He said to the boy, "La-Mont, why don't you quit staring and say 'hello' to Miss Nevada?"

LaMont's mouth gaped wide open as he continued to stare. When he finally gathered his composure, he asked in an incredulous voice, "Your last name is Nevada?"

PRISONERS OF OUR OWN CREATION

In our school, we have a "quiet" lunchroom. The cafeteria is located in the center of a slew of classrooms filled with students of various grades, so when one group is eating lunch, others are still in their rooms engaged in learning. The eaters must be quiet so as not to interrupt the learning process on the other side of the walls. The students have embraced the quiet lunchroom fully, and we now monitor it without an iron fist or threats of dismemberment, as the students eat with expedience so that they can be excused to go outside to yell and scream wildly.

Frequently, we share this aspect of our school with visitors (the quiet lunchroom, not the outside screaming), who are impressed and cannot wait to return to their schools to tell colleagues that it is indeed possible to conduct a lunch hour that does not breed chaos and mayhem.

One day, a student's grandmother walked through our lunchroom and developed a quite sour expression as she viewed the students eating. She walked over to where I was standing, and ignoring my outstretched hand as I introduced myself, she snarled, "I know who you are, and I don't like this one bit."

"Well, ma'am," I said as I kept my hand poised for a shake in case she changed her mind, "what exactly is it you have a problem with?"

"This lunchroom. The kids can't talk? What is this, jail? You should be ashamed of yourself. I was just visiting my son in prison, and even the prisoners are allowed to talk while they eat lunch. This is terrible."

"Well, ma'am," I smiled. "We keep them quiet and well disciplined with the expectation that they never have to go to prison. And if this state funded our schools at $30,000 per student like we pay per incarcerated individuals like your son, rather than at $5,000, we could buy a separate cafeteria and they could make all the noise they want during lunch."

I don't think she heard me say, "But thank you for your input," as she turned briskly away, leaving my outstretched hand waving in the breeze.

TIME TO FOCUS

As I explained in chapter 5, when a new principal comes on board, the staffers' expectations change, and there is a natural adjustment period. Sometimes, situations preempt the adjustment period, as the following pair of tales indicate.

First is the story of the teacher who thought that it would be okay to leave campus a half hour before the end of the school day, with students in her classroom, so that she could set up the food and drinks for the staff party she was hosting that night. When I walked into her room and she was not there, her partner teacher told me, "Um, she, well, she kind of left. Didn't she tell you?" Not only had she not told me, but she did not ask me, and I certainly would not have granted permission for her to shirk her teaching responsibilities for thirty extra minutes of setting out hors d'oeuvres.

Borderline irate, I returned to my office and stormed by my secretary, who called after me gingerly, "She wanted to tell you, but she couldn't find you. The old principal would let them do this, you know." I couldn't help but think, *If kids are the primary focus, how could a professional leave work while there are kids in the classroom?*

I phoned the teacher's house. There is a new sheriff in town. I left the following message on her answering machine in a rather stern voice: "Mrs. Shickendance, this is Mr. Hall at Anderson School. Please call me immediately." I don't think I put the phone down gently.

When the teacher returned the call five minutes later, her tail was tucked between her legs as she whimpered, "We had a lot of food to set up, and my partner was in the room. Do you want me to come back?" She had missed the point, but two things happened shortly thereafter: first, I did not attend the party, but I heard it was nice; second, she volunteered to go on our overage list so that she could return to work for her prior principal.

Second is the tale of the teacher assistant who wanted to be excused from work two afternoons per week to attend classes at the university. This would be perfectly acceptable if not for one glaring problem. She gets paid to work directly with students, and her allocation comes from the district and is nonnegotiable. She offered to make up the time after hours, but since her job is to work face-to-face with the children, that time is impossible to make up. I denied the request.

This decision got me in a lot of hot water with a faction of our parents, as the teacher assistant was a talented young Mexican American who had dreams of becoming a teacher. Although I was attacked by a lynch mob one morning after the morning music routine, I held fast. "We are a failing school," I told my area superintendent, when she questioned my decision. "We need people working directly with students, and I will not sacrifice several hours per week of a valuable district allocation to accommodate the individual desires of one staff member. It's not worth it to our kids."

To quote the rock band U2, "I don't believe in painted roses or bleeding hearts while bullets rape the night of the merciful." I equate that to the personal wishes and whines in the face of large percentages of illiterate students. I cannot, and I did not, allow my integrity to be compromised by outside pressure.

That teacher assistant quickly transferred to another school that had a schedule more accommodating of her needs.

A LITTLE UNION NEVER HURT ANYONE

After I recommended that the teacher I erroneously hired be dismissed midway through the school year (see the end of chapter 7), the folks down at the teachers' union erupted like Mount Saint Helens.

Although the dismissal was based primarily on the teacher's repeated acts of insubordination, there are other facts in play. She had been dismissed the previous year because of incompetence. She had earned an evaluation that contained over half of the teaching elements marked "Unsatisfactory" due to her demonstration of incompetence. The representative from the teachers' union, behind closed doors, told me, "We didn't go to bat for her last year, and we're not going to go to bat for her this year."

This changed when the head folks at the union office saw an opportunity to teach the new principal a lesson and strike fear in his heart. At the preliminary hearing, the focus of the union's argument had nothing, absolutely nothing, to do with the teacher in question, her glaring incompetence, and her blatant insubordinate acts. Rather, the entire ranting monologue had one purpose: crucify Mr. Hall. My integrity was questioned; my ability to conduct observations and follow the evaluation process was argued; my credibility was doubted; my leadership style was frowned on; my interpersonal respect was refuted; and my hairstyle was ridiculed. In short, I was drawn and quartered, tar and feathered, ripped up one side and down the other, and spiked on a spit like a four-hundred-pound hog, just without the apple. It was not pretty.

But, like always, I considered the source, remembered not to take this sort of weathering personally, and sat through the hearing, silently listening with a bemused look on my face, I'm sure. I was not intimidated, and I did not allow any vultures to feed on the mutilated pieces of my integrity. I remained stout.

As it turns out, teacher was suspended for insubordination and subsequently placed (through directed transfer) at another school. Our school survives; another surely suffers.

CLOSING THOUGHTS

This chapter would last forever if I were to write all the stories that transpired throughout the course of this first year, but then you wouldn't have time to collect your own. Did I mention we had a new fire alarm system installed in our school, and because of the asbestos abatement procedures, our school was uninhabitable for four of our five-week summer vacation? Or did I bring up the hullabaloo surrounding my decision to deny the continued request for two teachers to continue to split a contract by working half weeks each? How about the parent that came into the office, screaming and slamming doors, telling me I ought to call the police to protect myself? (I told him, "Why should I call the police? I'm not scared of you.")

There was the case of the parent who screamed into the phone, "I want to come down there and ring your little neck." I also recall the day we had a student threaten to kill several of his classmates with the rifle he uses to shoot squirrels . . . which happened to be the day the superintendent stopped by to observe a world-champion saddle bronc rider (that's a rodeo term, folks) speak to a group of our first graders. I might mention also that here I was, the youngest principal of the ninety school sites in our district, charged with the reconstruction of the only school in the state that failed to make "adequate yearly progress" for three consecutive years before my arrival. I could write another full book on the implementation and procedures of the change process, as our staff assessed our needs in the writing of a comprehensive school improvement plan . . . it goes on and on. But I'll stop here. You need to keep track of your own stories.

POINT TO PONDER

There are a million stories in the naked city. Start your collection now.

STAYING HEALTHY

He who fights with monsters might take care lest he thereby become a monster. Is not life a hundred times too short for us to bore ourselves?

—Friedrich Nietzsche

In the introduction, I made light of the fact that principals rank a close second to American presidents in the rate of gray hair growth during the job. It's no mystery that this is a stressful, anxiety-laden, hectic position in a complicated, dynamic, high-paced profession during a time of standards, public scrutiny, and accountability. The wear and tear of the daily toil can certainly take a toll on an individual's inner strength, physical and emotional health, attitude, and reserve tanks. It pays to stay healthy.

The following five suggestions are meant to establish a base of healthy options for the new principal of the new millennium. They require work on your part, but the work generally comprises dedication and persistence. Your efforts here will make your efforts in the office that much more manageable and meaningful.

Spend time away from work. You have a job that requires your supervision and physical presence for seven, eight, nine, or even more hours per day. You have paperwork and assorted other duties that constrict your time even further. When the work is done . . . leave! Get out of there. If you need to take a pile of evaluations home with you, do that. If you need to come in early tomorrow to finish a little project, do that. Don't grind yourself into the ground in any one day, because the week continues, the month goes on, and the year progresses whether you are in the office twelve hours per day or nine.

Do things for you. When you leave the building, go do something that you enjoy. Pick up a hobby. Do some crafts. Join a gym; get involved with city league softball, basketball, or badminton. Sew or paint; make ceramic ducks. Cook gourmet meals, play video games, visit the park with your kids. Walk the dog, chase rabbits, collect rainwater. Seek refuge and release in the activities that are personally rewarding, refreshing, and rejuvenating. The mental escape strengthens your emotional base, leaving you better equipped to face the challenges.

Don't take it personally. I have mentioned this before a couple of times, but it is worth repeating. This is a job. The principalship is a terribly demanding and challenging position. It is not easy, it is not smooth, and it is not always fun. Some people hate principals and have no trouble saying so. The principal is an easy target if things don't go well in a school. Get used to it, but don't let it erode your insides. When the going gets rough, detach yourself emotionally and proceed with the job.

Celebrate success. This goes for you, your family, your teaching staff, your students, your pets, and your neighborhood mail carrier. If something goes well, praise the people responsible and celebrate that success. Nothing improves morale more than knowing that someone took an interest in the good work you did. If you have to take an interest in your own good work, do so. It's okay to pat yourself on the back every now and then, and share those pats with the people that share this life with you. Like Kramer once rattled in a *Seinfeld* episode, "It's the feeling good all the time."

Eat away from your desk. Nothing ruins an appetite like a pile of work you know you really should be doing. Anxiety during eating increases your risk of stress-induced eating disorders and medical problems. Do you really want that, or would you rather eat that burrito in peace somewhere else? Research has shown that a typical office workstation (i.e., principal's desk) has more bacteria and germs than an average toilet seat. So . . . eat up or get up!

I'm not sure if I have made this clear, but the principalship is the world's most wonderful job. It's fantastic. The feeling of making a difference in a child's life is the most enlightening, meaningful feeling I can imagine.

I have the good fortune of being assigned to an outstanding school with a marvelous, truly dedicated teaching staff that is united in its goal of increasing student achievement. The test scores are just beginning to reflect our enthusiasm and commitment, and there is a palpable feel of positive energy exuding from this school, from front office to back classroom. I know we are doing right by our children.

It behooves me, then, to make an effort to maintain my physical and emotional health. My leadership as principal is the most influential aspect of this school. If I am not in tip-top shape, my impact in the education of our five hundred students becomes more at-risk than it already is. I cannot afford that, my teachers cannot afford that, and my students sure as hell cannot afford that.

So stay healthy . . . and go get 'em!

POINTS TO PONDER

- It pays to stay healthy. If you don't have your health, you have nothing at all. And this gig is the best job in the world; you don't want to miss a minute. Here are a few suggestions for how to stay healthy, both mentally and physically:
  - Spend time away from work. Get out of there, and don't even think about the job while you're gone. Most paperwork can wait.
  - Do things for you. Pick up a hobby, play sports, do some crafts, play with your children, take a class. Feed your inner self.
  - Don't take it personally. This is a job. You are a worker.
  - Celebrate success. No matter whose success it is, make a point to celebrate it publicly. This feeds and frees the soul.
  - Eat away from your desk. Eating and working are not compatible, so don't even try it. The work can wait until the food starts to digest.
- Enjoy. Remember: "It's a great life . . . if you don't weaken."

APPENDIXES

FORMS TO HELP
THE FIRST-YEAR PRINCIPAL

I am seeking, I am striving, I am in it with all my heart.

—Vincent Van Gogh

A

THE PRINCIPAL'S EIGHT-ROLE MONTHLY CHECKLIST

Instructions: Mark the box next to each item on the list to indicate that you performed that task during the past month. Then, below each item marked, give a concrete example or a clear explanation of that activity and its resultant effect.

❑ I encouraged at least one teacher to investigate and begin an action research project.
Details: _____

❑ I held a meeting to evaluate our writing/reading/math program.
Details: _____

❑ I researched a new method to assess student learning; I asked a teacher to try it and report back.
Details: _____

❑ I celebrated a teacher's (or student's) accomplishment publicly.
Details: _____

❑ I went to a conference, or I scheduled a presentation by a staff member who attended a conference.
Details: _____

Instructions: For each of the eight symbolic leadership roles that you adopted in the past month, mark the box. On the lines below, give a concrete example or clear explanation of that role and its resultant effect.

❑ *Historian:* probes into the past, discovering challenges, triumphs, and attempted change
   Details: _____

❑ *Anthropological sleuth:* researches and examines the school culture directly
   Details: _____

❑ *Visionary:* addresses and refines the school's mission and purpose
   Details: _____

❑ *Symbol:* defines the style and demeanor of the school
   Details: _____

❑ *Potter:* shapes the elements of the school culture with the vision in mind (the "pot")
   Details: _____

❑ *Poet:* uses words and images to evoke powerful emotional sentiments about the school
   Details: _____

❑ *Actor:* applies social dramas to reinforce cultural ties within the school community
   Details: _____

❑ *Healer:* helps in the change process by participating in ceremonies and commemorative events
   Details: _____

B

INTERVIEW QUESTIONS FOR PRINCIPALSHIP CANDIDATES

The following is a compilation of possible interview questions for a principalship candidate. I have also included the "hot topics" that you will want to review before any interviews, to solidify your viewpoints and philosophies. Your personal alignment helps your confidence and strength in relaying your views.

- Briefly tell us about yourself, how you got to where you are today, and why you are interested in being an administrator.
- What do you feel is your greatest accomplishment in life?
- What experiences have you had in managing schools in a site-based decision-making environment?
- How would you characterize your skills in communication, decision making, and conflict resolution?
- What are the ingredients of an exemplary school?
- In a financial pinch, when you are forced to reallocate staff, at what grade levels would you assign the larger class sizes, and why?
- Describe a school after five years with you as principal.
- Do you think social faculty functions are important? Why?
- What are your three best leadership qualities?
- How would you improve school–community relations?

- What are some ways that you would measure a teacher's effectiveness?
- What is the impact of inclusion on the school community?
- What would you do if an angry parent came in unexpectedly to demand that their child not be suspended for fighting?
- How would you describe the appearance of an effective classroom?
- What should a principal expect from teachers and staff?
- What is the most exciting thing going on in education today?
- Discuss the relationship between instructional improvement, teacher evaluation, and staff development.
- Suppose that several teachers have been grumbling in the lounge about lack of administrative support. What would you do?
- Name three books that have influenced you most in your professional career.
- How do you view negotiated employee contracts and the teachers' union?
- Why do you want to be a principal?

The following are "hot topics" with which your positions should be solid. Think about these seriously: record your philosophy and approach, and be sure of your thought process.

- Teachers and teacher quality
- Evaluations
- Students
- Instruction
- Discipline
- Community and parents
- School climate
- Budgets
- Leadership
- Core beliefs
- Strengths and weaknesses
- Effecting change
- At-risk and ESL education
- Effective reading program

C

SAMPLE AGENDA
FOR A STARTUP STAFF MEETING

This appendix contains the meeting agenda I used in my first year.

Our goal is to attain our ultimate potential. However, as our growth raises us toward this target, our potential expands. It is a never-ending quest to achieve an elusive objective, one with borderless capacity. The result is continual betterment of our selves along all fronts.

DAY ONE

Welcome

- Pick up goodies/handouts from entry table
- Pink information sheets/intelligence tests

Introductions

- Pete Hall, Principal
- Mr. Authority, Dean of Students/Math–Science Facilitator
- Partner introductions
- New staff on board

Change Is in the Air

- Natural, stressful, exciting
- New faces = new ideas, new conversations
- Change for the better

Our New Principal

- Children first—we will teach them to read
- "Always strive to be a better you."
- The Short List—what is nonnegotiable at Anderson School
- Communication: check e-mail daily
- Expectations: professional, role model, put forth your best

Programs

- We have a lot going on here at Anderson ES
- Title I, Title I "School Accountability" grant, NERA grant ($$)
- Success for All—Roots/Wings/Tutoring/Family Support (LC)
- NELIP/TLT (Lead teachers)
- ESL (Teachers), Special Education (Teachers)
- Computer Lab-on-Wheels (Computer Tech)
- Library (Librarian), Music (Teacher)
- Parent Involvement (PIF)
- Office business (Secretary)
- GUEST: Recycling (Plant Facilities)

Filling in the Blanks

- Master Calendar, Duty Schedule, Committees
- Computer lab/library/music schedules
- After-school programs need teachers: Twilight School, Homework Helpers

Discipline

- Supervision: active/vigilant
- Discipline with dignity
- Classroom plan—outline steps and consequences—documentation
- Citations, detention, office consequences

Safety

- Fire alarms, classroom pull-boxes
- Fire/evacuation drills
- Visitors (wanted or unwanted): Fences/gates 9:00–3:00
- Crossing guards, classroom supervision

Instruction

- Standards—plan books—grade books
- Lesson plan expectations—professional documentation
- Curriculum maps
- Classroom observations/formal vs. informal

Particulars

- Daily schedule, "The Week Ahead" notice
- All students exit through outside doors (at 3:00, no students are in the hallways)
- Certified evaluations
- Interruptions/intercom (Pledge of Allegiance?)
- Testing (security)
- Staff meetings
- Staff absences, substitute procedures (form, AESOP, folder)

Afternoon Goals

- School climate survey
- Lingering questions
- Work in classrooms: planning, organizing

DAY TWO

Business

- Answering lingering questions
- Student teacher request
- Do we have test-prep materials?

Discussion of School Choice Implications, AYP Formula . . .

Each school will be expected to make adequate yearly progress toward meeting state standards. This progress will be measured for all students by sorting test results for students who are economically disadvantaged, who are from racial or ethnic minority groups, who have disabilities, or who have limited English proficiency. The report cards will also sort results by gender and migrant status. Within twelve years, all students must perform at a proficient level under their state standards.

Results of Yesterday's Survey

The key values most important to us (as a group):

- Respect for others
- Responsibility
- Compassion
- Fairness
- Truth
- Self-respect

The values that are least important to us (as a group):

- Preservation of system
- Humility

CRT Graphs, Spring '02

Aligning curriculum and school decisions
    Accountability: we are all accountable to each other at all times.

Yesterday's List: Nonnegotiable Programs

SFA, ESL, Special Ed, Computers, Library, Music, Kitchen, Parent Involvement, Custodians, NELIP/TLT, Sunshine Books . . .

Today's List: Everything Else—Let's Prioritize

Think rocks, pebbles, sand, and water.

Grade-Level/Specialty-Area Meetings

Rough scope and sequence for all grade levels: (1) language arts, (2) math, (3) science, (4) social studies

Lunch

Murrietta's Restaurant and Cantina, 4385 Neil Road (Neil and Peckham) 11:30 AM, my treat

D

INTERVIEW QUESTIONS FOR TEACHER CANDIDATES

Name: _____ Date: _____ Time: _____

1. Tell us a bit about your recent work experience and why you would be interested in working here at Anderson School.

   _____

   _____

   _____

2. Of our student population, 85 percent live at or below the poverty level, and over half of our students are native Spanish speakers. What experiences have you had working with at-risk or ESL students, and how could you draw on those experiences to help you acclimate to working at this school?

   _____

   _____

   _____

3. This school has adopted Success for All as one of its primary tools for teaching reading. Are you familiar with SFA, and are you willing to commit to the training and the time it takes to prepare daily?

   _____

   _____

   _____

4. Those who work for me know that classroom management is a major focus. Explain for us how you will develop standards of student conduct to maintain order and discipline in your class.

   _____

   _____

   _____

5. Name the five key elements of literacy and give us a brief example of how you would teach each one to a struggling student.

   _____

   _____

   _____

6. What special skills or talents would you bring to Anderson? How would the school community benefit from your presence?

   _____

   _____

   _____

7. I'm going to come visit your classroom on the first day of school. What am I going to see during those first two hours of school?

   _____

   _____

   _____

8. Tell us three to five characteristics that describe you as a person and as a teacher.

   _____

   _____

   _____

9. That about wraps it up. Do you have any questions for us?

   _____

   _____

   _____

Obervation Items (circle one)

Professional image:

   excellent   good   average   poor

Interpersonal skills:
    excellent   good   average   poor

Communication skills:
    excellent   good   average   poor

Professional Items (circle one)

Demonstrates knowledge of subject matter/curriculum:
    excellent   good   average   poor

Displays understanding of positive/strong student management techniques:
    excellent   good   average   poor

Provides opportunities for individual differences:
    excellent   good   average   poor

Demonstrates ability to motivate students:
    excellent   good   average   poor

Overall rating (circle one):
    excellent   good   average   poor

Notes and comments:

_____

_____

_____

Interviewer's name: _____

E

WALK-THROUGH CHECKLIST

*U*se this checklist when conducting classroom walk-throughs.

Name: _____ Date: _____ Time: _____

Subject: _____

Format:
- ❑ Whole class
- ❑ Teams
- ❑ Partners
- ❑ Individual
- ❑ TTYP
- ❑ Team points

Content: _____

Learning objective: _____

What is the teacher doing?

_____

_____

_____

_____

What are the students doing?

_____

_____

_____

_____

Comments: _____

_____

_____

_____

_____

F

POSTOBSERVATION SELF-REFLECTION FORM FOR TEACHERS

Leave this form for teachers after a lesson.

Please take the time to reflect on the lesson, then complete this form. Bring the completed form to the postconference meeting with Mr. Hall.

Name: _____ Date: _____ Time: _____

1. To what extent were the students productively engaged? How can I tell?

   _____
   _____
   _____

2. Did the students learn what I intended? Were my instructional goals met? How do I know?

   _____
   _____
   _____

3. Which students did (or did not) meet the instructional goals? Why (or why not)?

   _____

   _____

   _____

4. Did I alter my goals or instructional plan as I taught the lesson? If so, why?

   _____

   _____

   _____

5. If I had the opportunity to teach this lesson again to this same group of students, what would I do differently? Why?

   _____

   _____

   _____

6. Review several samples of student work on this assignment. What feedback did I (or will I) provide to students on their work?

   _____

   _____

   _____

7. What other information would be helpful to know in contemplating this lesson?

   _____

   _____

   _____

Teacher's signature/date: _____

G

BELIEF SYSTEM QUESTIONNAIRE

*U*se this before the start of the school year and compare the results with those you collect at the end of the school year.

Note: This is an instrument for gathering information. Please answer with complete honesty.

Directions: Look at the list of fifteen values carefully. Check the values that are most important to you in your daily work and in your daily life. Then circle the value you consider to be most important.

Compassion	Honor	Reverence for life
Devotion	Humility	Self-respect
Fairness	Preservation of system	Social harmony
Freedom	Respect for others	Tolerance
Generosity	Responsibility	Truth

Directions: Using the scale below, indicate how important each of the following goals is to you.

1 = Extremely important   2 = Very important
3 = Average importance   4 = Not important

1. Increasing basic skills of students (reading, writing, and math)

　　　　　　　　　　　　　　　　　　　　　　1　2　3　4

2. Increasing the breadth of topics covered (health, art, science, PE, etc.)　　　　　　　　　　　　　　　　1　2　3　4

3. Enhancing extracurricular activities (sports, clubs, intramural programs, etc.)　　　　　　　　　　　　1　2　3　4

4. Upgrading staff development and in-service programs

　　　　　　　　　　　　　　　　　　　　　　1　2　3　4

5. Increasing the cost effectiveness of the school's programs

　　　　　　　　　　　　　　　　　　　　　　1　2　3　4

6. Upgrading the physical resources of the school　　1　2　3　4

7. Developing better policies and procedures to maximize instructional time　　　　　　　　　　　　　1　2　3　4

8. Upgrading programs for special ed, gifted, or low-functioning students　　　　　　　　　　　　　　1　2　3　4

9. Upgrading discipline plans and practices　　　1　2　3　4

10. Increasing parent/community involvement　　1　2　3　4

Directions: Using the scale below, indicate your level of agreement with the following statements.

1 = Strongly agree　　　2 = Agree　　　3 = Neutral
4 = Disagree　　　　　　5 = Strongly disagree

11. I believe our purpose in school is to prepare our students for society.　　　　　　　　　　　　1　2　3　4　5

12. I believe all students, every one of them, can learn.

　　　　　　　　　　　　　　　　　　　　　1　2　3　4　5

13. I believe there is no right way to teach every child.

　　　　　　　　　　　　　　　　　　　　　1　2　3　4　5

14. I believe I will never know everything I need to know.

　　　　　　　　　　　　　　　　　　　　　1　2　3　4　5

15. I believe professional development is crucial to school improvement.　　　　　　　　　　　　　1　2　3　4　5

16. I believe diversity enhances the school community positively.

　　　　　　　　　　　　　　　　　　　　　1　2　3　4　5

17. I believe keeping teachers happy will make my job easier.

    1   2   3   4   5

18. I believe keeping parents happy will make my job easier.

    1   2   3   4   5

19. I believe children should be the focal point in all school decisions.

    1   2   3   4   5

20. I believe rocking the boat will eventually make it tip and sink.

    1   2   3   4   5

21. I believe how I look and act influences everyone in the school community.

    1   2   3   4   5

22. I believe some teachers are ineffective and unable to change.

    1   2   3   4   5

23. I believe people will rise to the expectations set for them.

    1   2   3   4   5

H

PRINCIPAL PERFORMANCE
QUESTIONNAIRE

*U*se this at the conclusion of the school year to obtain honest, real feed-back from your staff.

Note: This was my first year as principal, and I'm glad to have spent it at Anderson. Now, you know I have a proclivity toward data collection and analysis—in other words, I like data. I don't need pats on the back or feigned exuberance, but I can respect some honest, detailed feedback.

Directions: Please answer these questions honestly and openly, without fear of reprisal or indignation. My goal is to help make Anderson School the best it can be, plain and simple. Compliments may make me blush, but criticisms will not hurt my feelings.

1. When you tell your friends/spouse/dog about your principal, what do you tell them?

   _____

   _____

   _____

2. Do you feel Mr. Hall makes decisions based on what is best for our students? What makes you think that way?

_____

_____

_____

3. When you disagreed with a school policy or a decision made by Mr. Hall, what did you do about it? Was the problem resolved? How so?

_____

_____

_____

4. How would you describe the climate at Anderson School this year?

_____

_____

_____

5. What are the three areas of the school operation we should focus on the most next year?

_____

_____

_____

6. What are your suggestions for improving those three areas?

_____

_____

_____

7. Name three things that regard Anderson School or that happened this year that make you proud.

_____

_____

_____

8. Any other notes/comments/questions/concerns:

_____

_____

_____

ANNOTATED REFERENCES

As you embark on this noble quest, you may find any of the books in the following list helpful. Of course, hundreds of other texts are intended for a similar audience, so consider these as simply a starting point.

Blanchard, K., W. Oncken, Jr., and H. Burrows. 1989. *The One-Minute Manager Meets the Monkey*. New York: William Morrow.

This could very well be the bible of delegation and management guides. The authors share their expert opinion on how to empower employees and avoid taking on more than your share.

Clark, R. 2003. *The Essential 55: An Award-Winning Teacher's Rules for Discovering the Successful Student in Every Child*. New York: Hyperion.

Mr. Clark, the 2001 Disney Teacher of the Year, wrote this book to share his message with the world. Now you can share it with your teaching staff. What a terrific gift this would make to help remind teachers why we're in the busines and what our effect can be!

Connors, N. A. 2000. *If You Don't Feed the Teachers, They Eat the Students*. Nashville, Tenn.: Incentive Publications.

This clever, insightful text is full of energy and suggestions for empowering and getting the most out of the people who work for you. This is written specifically with school administrators in mind.

Danielson, C., and T. McGreal. 2000. *Teacher Evaluation to Enhance Professional Practice*. Princeton, N.J.: Educational Testing Service.

Distributed by the Association for Supervision and Curriculum Development, this book provides the foundation on which my school district (and many others nationwide) bases its teacher evaluation system. It outlines the expectations, philosophy, and specific practices for evaluating school personnel.

DuFour, R., and R. Eacker. 1998. *Professional Learning Communities at Work: Best Practices for Enhancing Student Achievement*. Bloomington, Ind.: NES.

These authors outline a philosophical approach to school improvement through the creation of a professional learning community. This book provides good examples, great ideas, and some useful strategies to employ immediately with a teaching staff.

Gurian, M. 1996. *The Wonder of Boys: What Parents, Mentors and Educators Can Do to Shape Boys into Exceptional Men*. New York: Tarcher/Putnam.

Dr. Gurian shares his professional knowledge as a therapist and educator, regarding the peculiar needs, propensities, and characteristics of boys in today's world. As we deal with boys all day, every day, this is particularly relevant to the field of education.

Monroe, L. 1997. *Nothing's Impossible*. New York: Public Affairs.

This is Dr. Lorraine Monroe's tale of turning a flailing inner-city school in Harlem into a beacon called the Douglass Academy, now one of the finest schools in the country. Combining an honest look at educational leadership with rules and stories, this is a must-read for any administrator.

Schmoker, M. 1999. *Results: The Key to Continuous School Improvement*. Alexandria, Va.: ASCD.

An established professional educational consultant, the author shares methods of evaluating schools, programs, instruction, and reform, with specific guidelines and many real-life examples from the field.